FEELING GOOD THERAPY

A Practical Guide with Strategies to Fight Pessimism, Anxiety, Low Self-Esteem and Other Disorders to Feel Better Every Day, Benefits Of Mindfulness

DANIEL CHARISMA ROY WENDLER BRIGGS

TABLE OF CONTENTS

Introduction 2

Chapter 1 6

   Feeling Good 7

   The Different Areas Of Well-Being 13

Chapter 2: When You Don't Feel Good 33

   Factors That Affect Well-Being 33

   The Impact Of Negative Well-Being On Life 37

Chapter 3: Negative Emotions And Disorders 46

   Depression 47

   Anxiety 51

   Post-Traumatic Stress Disorder 57

   Low Self-Esteem 59

   Pessimism 63

   Why Kindness Is Important 64

Chapter 4: Shifting The Mindset 68

   What Is The Mindset 68

   Shifting Your Mindset 71

   How To Level Up Your Mindset 75

   Embrace Change Through A New Mindset 78

   Developing A New Habit 81

   How To Stop Being A Victim 85

Change Your Circle And Change Your Mindset 89

Chapter 5: The Power Of Self-Care 102

Benefits Of Self-Care 102

How To Engage In Self-Care 105

Mindfulness 109

Decluttering 116

The Benefits Of Exercise 118

Sleep Better At Night 121

Volunteering And Why It Makes You Feel Good ..126

Stress Management Techniques 129

Chapter 6: When To Get Professional Help 133

Stigma Of Asking For Help 134

Why Vulnerability Is Strength 138

How To Make Yourself Vulnerable 142

What Is A Life Coach? 147

What Is A Licensed Therapist? 153

A Psychologist Vs. Psychiatrist 161

Chapter 7: The Advantages Of Feeling Good 163

Feeling Good At Work 164

Happiness Leads To Health 166

Feeling Good And Relationships 170

The Law Of Attraction 173

The Ways To Approach Life 176

Chapter 8: Feeling Good In Real Life 179
- Mike's Story 179
- Jennifer's Story 182
- Sam's Story 186

Conclusion 190

© Copyright 2020 by DANIEL CHARISMA ROY WENDLER BRIGGS. All right reserved.

The work contained herein has been produced with the intent to provide relevant knowledge and information on the topic on the topic described in the title for entertainment purposes only. While the author has gone to every extent to furnish up to date and true information, no claims can be made as to its accuracy or validity as the author has made no claims to be an expert on this topic. Notwithstanding, the reader is asked to do their own research and consult any subject matter experts they deem necessary to ensure the quality and accuracy of the material presented herein.

This statement is legally binding as deemed by the Committee of Publishers Association and the American Bar Association for the territory of the United States. Other jurisdictions may apply their own legal statutes. Any reproduction, transmission or copying of this material contained in this work without the express written consent of the copyright holder shall be deemed as a copyright violation as per the current legislation in force on the date of publishing and subsequent time thereafter. All additional works derived from this material may be claimed by the holder of this copyright.

The data, depictions, events, descriptions and all other information forthwith are considered to be true, fair and accurate unless the work is expressly described as a work of fiction. Regardless of the nature of this work, the Publisher is exempt from any responsibility of actions taken by the reader in conjunction with this work. The Publisher acknowledges that the reader acts of their own accord and releases the author and Publisher of any responsibility for the observance of tips, advice, counsel, strategies and techniques that may be offered in this volume.

Introduction

Congratulations on purchasing (Topic: *Feeling Good Therapy),* and thank you for doing so. If you ask most people if they would like to feel good, we can expect the answer in most cases to be a resounding yes. Most people do not actively want to feel bad, even if their actions might suggest otherwise. The confusion here is that many people do not know what it means to feel good, or if they do, have no idea how to reach that state of mind. This is what I am here to help you, the reader, figure out today.

The focus of this book will be to discuss feeling good therapy and what it means in your life. It feels good to feel good, and I will go over the many ways it can be done through many different strategies, techniques, and action plans.

The following chapters will discuss what feeling good means in every aspect of our lives, including physical, mental, emotional, and spiritual. All of these areas make up who we are, and it is important to take care of all of them to become fully and completely healthy individuals—feeling good can personal in many ways, so I will be addressing this topic in the general sense and focusing on many of the signs of what feeling good looks like, both on the inside and out.

Furthermore, I will discuss what it means to not feel good. This will include the many signs and symptoms of a person who is going through the process of not feeling good and the damaging effects it has on them in every aspect of their lives. Our career, personal lives, relationships, and health rely on whether or not we feel good on a regular basis. There are certainly days we will feel better than others, but the goal is to feel good most of the time.

Many negative emotions and mood disorders can lead to the feelings we have been discussing, and this book will get into all of those, as well. Mood disorders and mental health issues have plagued society for generations. However, they were not taken very seriously in the past. Lucky for us, this is changing slowly, but we still have a lot of progress that needs to be made.

A lot of how we feel is determined by the mindset that we carry. Our mindset and the way we think play a huge role in how we feel about ourselves and the world around us. Unfortunately, many people are walking around with a poor mindset and do not even realize it. Part of this book will focus on shifting the mindset towards the positive and the impact this will have on how we feel. Changing our mindset will eventually lead to changing our mood, thoughts, actions, and result. It will create a positive cascade of events leading to us feeling good overall.

Besides changing our mindset, self-care is also an important aspect of feeling good. Many of us become so busy with all of the requirements of life and helping other people that we forget to take care of the most important person, ourselves. Self-care is simple enough to do but difficult for many people to make a habit out of. A major focus here will be the importance of self-care and how to make it an essential part of our lives. Specific self-care activities will also be discussed to give readers some examples to follow.

In some cases, feeling good becomes so far out of our reach that we cannot see it or obtain it. In these cases, we may need the help of a professional to guide us in the right direction and find the happiness we need to feel good. I will go over the different types of professionals that are available, like life coaches and licensed therapists, and when it is appropriate to see which one.

Finally, I will bring it all together by discussing why it's important to feel good. Our mood plays a major role in how we view the world, and therefore, how our lives turn out. There are many reasons that you want to feel good. There will be many advantages to gain from this, and every section of our lives will be affected positively. Basically, it feels good to feel good, and we should strive for this as much as possible. Once you have this feeling on a regular basis, you will have the ability to start living the life you desire.

People underestimate how much their mood actually affects them. However, waking up, living your day, and going to bed with a positive attitude will mean a lot towards gaining the success you want in life. Feeling good therapy works by giving us true happiness, and my hope is that all of you will understand what it is and strive to achieve it.

There are plenty of books on this subject on the market, thanks again for choosing this one! Every effort was made to ensure it is full of as much useful information as possible. Please enjoy!

Chapter 1: What Does Feeling Good Mean?

There is no simple answer here when referring to feeling good or feeling good therapy. Honestly, it is a subjective state to be based on what makes a person happy in every possible way. Some individuals refer to feeling good as living the life they enjoy. Many people value a good career, extensive family time, health, or a combination of both. There are those who love to travel and be wanderlusts their whole lives, while others are happily taking a trip once a year. Furthermore, many people just like to stay home and never leave their familiar surroundings.

When we are trying to define what feeling good means, it is quite complicated in the sense that there is no single answer. It is very individualized. However, I can try to explain it in the general sense. When referring to feeling good, we generally mean being in a positive state of well-being, which includes having good mental and physical health, having a sense of purpose, low or manageable stress, and just feeling happy, overall. According to the

Oxford English Dictionary, well-being is defined as the state of being comfortable, happy, and healthy.

Positive well-being is something that is sought out by everyone. People want to feel good; however, their thoughts and actions can tell a different story. Nonetheless, nobody really wakes up and tells themselves it's great to be miserable. They just don't know how to be happy or realize how their thoughts and actions affect them. The focus of this chapter will be to thoroughly describe what well-being, or feeling good, means from all aspects of our lives.

Feeling Good

Feeling good means that you have a constant flow of positive energy. This energy flow is not just from the big things in life, like career, but small miracles that occur every day. The little things in life that bring us joy are what matter most to us in the end. Unfortunately, many of us take those for granted because we don't realize their immense impact. However, in the long run, we end up missing the little things, as opposed to the big things. For example, waking up in the morning after a good night's sleep, eating your favorite meals, and spending time with good people make more of an impact in your life than many of the big events. Yes, the big things are goals that we are after, but the little things keep us moving every day. The everyday things are what make us feel good.

The following are a few main dimensions of life that will contribute to a sustained state of well-being.

Self-Accepting Beliefs

Beliefs play a significant role in how we see the world, and what we believe about ourselves is a key factor in our well-being. Self-accepting beliefs are important because they provide programming at the subconscious level that points towards feeling good. If your beliefs are not self-accepting, then you will usually go into distress. It takes a while to develop these beliefs to the point that they enter our subconscious mind, so the sooner you can start incorporating positive words into your vocabulary. The following are examples of specific beliefs that can help with your overall well-being:

- I am a lovable person, and there is no reason for people not to like me.
- I am attractive, despite what people tell me.
- I am capable of great things and success.
- For the most part, things work out well for me, and I have a pretty good life.
- I know I am not perfect, but I am good the way I am.
- Other people's opinions about me do not matter as much as my own.
- I am deserving of happiness, just like anyone else.

- I am smart and can accomplish what I set out to do.
- Other people's negative opinions of me don't matter if I don't believe them.

If you have a tendency to harbor negative views about yourself and everything around you, you can start changing these views. You decide how you feel. I will get into more detail about mindset shifts later in this book.

Self-Accepting Beliefs

Circumstances

The circumstances we find ourselves in play a huge role in our well-being too. This can include money woes, illnesses, poor living conditions, and hostile or unpleasant people in our lives. Anything that extreme adversity to the point where it's unmanageable can undermine well-being, especially if these pose a threat to survival. For example, living in a dangerous neighborhood.

Psychologist Abraham Maslow placed the need for security at a hierarchy on his pyramid. Humans need to feel secure in their lives, which is why they seek out shelter, become aware in public places, lock their doors, and take many other precautionary measures for their safety. The safer you feel in every aspect, the better your well-being is.

Relationships

If you are like most people, healthy relationships are essential for you as positive interactions provide a feeling of safety and social enrichment. A lack of social interactions, even for introverts, can create a sense of loneliness.

Yes, positive interactions with close friends and family are needed in times like these, even if it's for a short while. However, even getting out of the house and being in a public area, like a store or park, can make someone feel better in this regard. Being around others who are also living their lives can make you realize that you are not alone in this world.

On the other hand, relationships can also be the cause of a lack of well-being. Being around negative people all the time, whether you know them well or not, can prove to be detrimental to your psyche. These types of relationships will make you spiral down rather than lift you up.

Activities You Enjoy

What do you spend your day doing? Do you go to work, come home, do household chores, take care of family, and then go to bed? All of these tasks are essential, but what I am concerned about is what you do during your downtime after your responsibilities have been taken care of. Do you spend these hours doing something for yourself, or are you busy taking care of other people's needs? If it is the latter, then you have some serious work to do.

Being able to spend time doing the things you love is essential for your well-being. This includes saying no to activities you don't want to do. For example, if you have had a long day and just want to sit at home and relax, then you have the right to do so. You are not obligated to go out if someone invites you. You can respectfully decline because what you want to do is important too.

In relationships, especially committed ones, one party is often quick to concede on what they want because they believe that is the norm. However, a relationship needs to be an equal partnership with a compromise, so all those involved can feel a sense of well-being. If one partner chose the activity one week, the other partner would choose it the following week. How much time do you spend on the things you love? If your answer is along the lines of not enough, then you need to start changing things.

Gratitude

Gratitude is a great way to get rid of distress. When you start expressing gratitude, then you begin focusing on all of the good things you have instead of the negative things or what's missing. Instead of spending your time thinking about the negative aspects of your life, start being grateful for the positive areas. If you think hard enough, you will always find something good in your life that will make you realize things are not as bad as they appeared. You can show gratitude by:

- Saying thank you to people, even for the smallest things.
- Doing a gratitude ritual where you stop for a moment and remember all of the things you are grateful for.
- Do something kind for another person, which will help you realize the value you bring to the world.
- Write down all of your accomplishments.
- Take yourself out on a date. This means going out to do something you love all by yourself.
- Write yourself a love letter where you put down all of the things you admire about yourself. This can literally be anything.

- Praise people whenever they do something good. This does not have to be anything major. Even small acts deserve some praise.

The Different Areas of Well-Being

Feeling good is not just related to what can be seen on the outside. It refers to every aspect of our being. If one section of our lives is not going well, then the others will suffer too. While we can never be perfect, we can certainly create a life where things are as balanced as possible. In this section, I will provide an overview of what well-being is in all of the major areas of our lives.

Physical Well-being

Physical well-being is the ability to improve the functioning of your body through healthy practices, like eating well, getting proper sleep, and exercising regularly. When people are more physically healthy, they can do everything else in their lives better. They will have more energy, focus, discipline, and determination to get things done. With our busy, stressed-out lives, we tend to put physical health on the backburner, even though it is one of the most important factors to pay attention to. It needs to be something we prioritize and put to the forefront of our minds.

Why do people ignore it if it's so crucial? Well, we have already mentioned one of the reasons, and that is time.

Time is a finite resource, and we can only spend certain amounts of it engaging in specific activities. Unfortunately, those activities often not what's best for us. Instead of health and wellness, we choose to work excessive hours, spending time on social media, binge-eating junk food instead of preparing healthy meals, or spending time with people we would rather not be around.

There is a lot of complicated information out there regarding the creation of health and happiness. People fall in love with new fads, like diets or workouts. They want a quick-fix instead of putting in regular effort to make themselves feel good. The truth is, being in a state of physical well-being is a lifelong pursuit. It does not happen overnight and lasts forever. Major lifestyle changes are required, which must be followed routinely. To make it simple, the following are some essential areas to pay attention to if you want to start feeling good physically

Sleep

Unless you are one of the outliers who does not require much sleep, it is generally recommended to get about seven to eight hours of good rest. This will help you stay healthy and alert. The key is the sleep must be good and peaceful. If you are tossing and turning, waking up frequently, and never feel fully rested when you wake up, then your sleep patterns are an issue. You are not getting a restful night's sleep. Look at the factors that might be causing this. For example, are you taking in too much caffeine or sugar throughout the day? Are you eating a heavy meal or imbibing extra alcohol right before bed? Are you playing on your phone, tablet, or computer? Are you watching TV and falling asleep with it on?

While some of these activities may seem minor, they can result in poor sleep habits. They will likely affect your deep sleep, so you never get to fully rest. Furthermore, not having a routine sleep schedule can also be a negative factor. If you fall asleep at 10 PM on weekdays and 3 AM during the weekend, your sleep cycle will be thrown off, and your body clock will get confused. It will not know when it's time to rest and when it's time to be energetic. As a result, you will be tired during the day and have a hard time sleeping during the night.

If your sleep habits are not good, you will be plagued with fatigue, lethargy, poor performance, memory issues, irritability, higher stress levels, and increased risk of chronic illnesses. People disregard how much a lack of rest can lead to a poor immune system.

Eating Well

Contrary to popular belief, eating healthy does not mean only ingesting grass or starving yourself every day. Ironically, these are actually very unhealthy habits. Eating well refers to taking in food with the proper nutrient density. This means you are getting an adequate amount of essential nutrients that are needed to power up your metabolic processes. You will never feel hungry; however, you will also not feel bloated or excessively full. There will be a balance between the two.

The problem with many diet plans is that they deprive your body of many nutrients they need, and therefore, your body is always craving them. Eventually, they will get them from the wrong source. While everyone is different as far as their physiological processes, the following is a quick rundown of the essential food groups to include in your meal plans:

- Fruits and vegetables
- Whole grains and nuts
- Lean meats and poultry
- Fish that are rich in Omega-3 fatty acids
- Healthy fats like olive oil or avocado oil
- Coffees and Teas, especially black coffee and green tea
- Drink plenty of water

Avoid foods with too much sugar, cholesterol, and unhealthy fats, like vegetable oil, butter, or lard. Many fried foods, packaged snacks, frozen treats, and baked goods contain excess amounts of unhealthy ingredients.

Having a well-balanced diet can be amazing for your physical health. Do not skip meals or try to starve yourself to lose weight. This will only confuse your body and slow down your metabolism. Plus, it will make you lethargic, angry, and unproductive. You need to eat, but the key is to always eat well. Also, avoid overeating because this can have many metabolic consequences too. Your metabolism can have a hard time keeping up and lead to you storing extra fat in places it does not need to go.

Believe it or not, unhealthy food does not have to taste bad. There are plenty of healthy options if you just look close enough. The key is to make sure you are getting all of your essential nutrients, like proteins, fats, carbohydrates, vitamins, and minerals.

Healthy Eating

Physical Activity

Physical activity and getting up to move around is a major contributor to physical well-being. Many people have a plethora of bad memories or negative opinions about exercise. Perhaps they were not great during gym class in high school; they were constantly picked last for every sports team, they hated going to the gym, or they run awkwardly. There are many reasons exercise can elicit poor responses, and people will avoid it at all costs.

My question is, why does exercise have to be any of the above things? Any type of physical activity is okay, and everyone can find some reason and way to get up and start moving. If you like to run, go for a run. If you are a gym rat, then go to the gym. If you love playing basketball, racquetball, softball, or bowling, engage in one of these activities. There are plenty of home workouts for you to do. Also, you can just stand up and begin jogging in place. There are no specific rules for physical activity. Find what you love to do and start moving.

The long-term benefits of exercise are undeniable. Getting your blood flowing and your muscles moving is a great way to lose weight, gain energy, focus your mind, reduce stress, and avoid many chronic illnesses like obesity, diabetes, blood pressure, or heart disease. Plus, building up a sweat makes you feel fairly good. Still, people have a hard time incorporating an exercise routine into their schedule. Much of this has to do with discipline. The last thing many individuals want to do is put on workout clothes and start exercising.

This is why it's important to fit physical activity into your schedule in a way that is convenient for you. You can wake up earlier and do it first thing in the morning or in the evening after work. Also, you can make physical activity a part of your normal routine. For example, if you are going to the store, instead of driving, walk or ride a bike. Instead of elevators, take the stairs. Substitute modern conveniences for old school methods where it is applicable, and you will notice yourself moving a lot more.

No matter how much you deny it, physical activity and exercise are essential for well-being. Sitting around all day being inactive will do you no good in the long run. You will into a rut with low energy and poor performance, in general. Decide what routines you enjoy and find time to engage in them.

Hygiene

Hygiene is defined as any action taken to maintain health and prevent disease. It goes beyond just brushing your teeth or taking a shower. Personal hygiene activities not only improve your health but boost your mood, as well. Taking a good shower after a long day can help you rest better at night and also get you going in the morning.

Besides personal care at home, hygiene also includes preventative care, like going to the doctor or dentist for regular checkups. People often put these off because of convenience and also being worried about getting and news. I will tell you now that finding a problem early is much better than finding out too late when it's much harder to prevent complications. Not ignoring your health concerns is a significant part of proper hygiene practices.

Relaxation

Believe it or not, you are allowed to relax once in a while. It is okay to sit on your couch after a long day of work and not have to do countless chores. There's no problem with actually enjoying your weekend. You can go on vacation and use it to decompress, rather than fill up your day with activities. Relaxation is a major contributor to well-being because we need moments to sit down and recharge our batteries. If you don't, we will burnout and fall apart soon enough.

While it's good to be ambitious, always remember that your body can only handle so much. You are not a machine that is meant to be on the move all the time. When you are packing up your schedule in your planner, block off some time for fun activities and make sure you stick to them. These activities can be anything you want, like watching a movie, sitting by the pool, going for a hike, spending time with friends, or getting out of town for a while. When you are relaxing, make sure your mind is fully focused on it.

Mental Well-Being

The next important aspect of feeling good is our mental well-being. This refers to how well we can respond to the ups and downs of life. We cannot control life, but we can certainly control what happens to us. Some examples include:

- A person losing their job because of a poor economy but uses this opportunity to takes some classes and develop new skills that will help them in the long run. Eventually, a new career path becomes available based on what the individuals have just learned.
- A man goes through a major divorce because his wife cheats on him. However, he decided to move on and handle things civilly, so he can continue living with happiness.
- A woman was once homeless, but once she gets herself out of this situation, she goes back to help those who are in the position she was once in.

The components of mental well-being are within everyone's reach. This can be true whether there is a mental health illness involved or not. The following are some steps anyone can take in order to start improving their mental well-being.

Connect With Other People

Good relationships are especially important for mental health. The people we keep around us determine the type of mood we will be in. Connecting with good people can:

Help you build a sense of belonging and self-worth.

Give you an opportunity to share positive experiences.

Provide a lot of emotional support and allow you to support other people.

Give you comfort in knowing people have your back.

Your circle does not have to be large, but it must be strong. Those who try to threaten your mental well-being should be distanced from as much as possible. There are several things you can do to try and build a stronger relationship:

- If possible, take time each day to be around your family. Block off time every day, just like you would anything else on your schedule. For example, dinner time can always be spent eating together, or you can all watch movies at the end of the night. Weekends, or other days off, can be used for bonding moments, whatever they might be.

- Arrange a day out with friends that you enjoy being around. You don't have to do anything extravagant on these days; you just have to be together.
- Switch off the news, social media, or anything else you get negative information from. Instead, use your energy to spend time with your kids or other people you don't see often.
- Have lunch with a colleague and discuss things that are not work-related.
- Volunteer in your community, like at a church, school, hospital, or some type of community center.
- Make use of technology to stay connected with friends all over the world. Before, it was difficult to keep in touch with people once they moved away. Now, it is hard not to. With a simple message or video call, you can easily connect with anyone across the globe.

Look for those real-life human connections. When you find them, you will greatly improve your mental well-being.

Be Physically Active

Being physically active is not just great for your physical well-being, but your mental well-being also. There is much evidence that suggests getting up and moving around greatly reduces stress and promotes happiness. Being physically active can:

- Raise your self-esteem.
- Help you become better at setting goals and overcoming challenges. When you set personal fitness goals, you learn how to perform this function for other areas of your life too.
- Cause chemical changes in your brain that result in positive mood changes.
- I discussed how to incorporate physical activity into your daily routine, but just to recap:
- Find activities that you love to do and engage in them.
- In lieu of getting expensive gym memberships, you can find free activities like running, riding your bike, going for a walk, hiking, or getting involved in community programs.
- Develop the discipline to get up and get moving every day, no matter how busy you are.

Learn New Skills

Learning new skills is a great way to improve your mental well-being. For those of you wondering, yes, you do have time. Assess your schedule and remove certain activities that are bringing you no value. Instead, use this time to learn something new. It does not have to be towards a new career. It can simply be a hobby you enjoy partaking in. New skills will improve your mental well-being by:

- Boosting your self-confidence and raising your self-esteem. Whenever you gain new knowledge, it makes you feel better about yourself.
- Helping you build a sense of purpose.
- Allowing you to connect with new people who you may have never met otherwise.

There are many paths you can take to learn a new skill, including:

- Learning how to cook a new dish, whether it's from a class, a book, a video, or through experimentation.
- Taking on a new responsibility at work, like a new project, mentoring a coworker, or getting a promotion.
- Work on projects at home, like the yard, basement, or bedroom. Figure out small improvements you can make and try fixing them yourself.
- Learn a new language.
- Sign up for a course at your local college.
- You could attend a trade school to possibly learn a skill for a new career path.
- Attend seminars on topics you are interested in.
- Take on a new hobby that will challenge.

This new activity you take on does not have to be cumbersome. It does not even have to be a skill you will ever use again. It can just be something you take on for the sake of learning.

Give to Others

Acts of giving and kindness can also improve your mental well-being. When you give to others, it helps put your own circumstances in perspective. Plus, it makes it obvious that you bring some value to the world. Giving to others can improve your mental well-being in the following manner:

- Creating positive feelings and a sense of reward. The joy you get from helping other people in their time of need is irreplaceable.
- Giving you a sense of purpose and self-worth. When you are all able to help someone who needs it, it is very satisfying and makes you feel like you've made a difference.
- Helps you connect with other people.
- Helps you learn what the important things in this world are.

You don't have to donate large sums of money or spend your entire time volunteering. Small acts of kindness can go a long way. Some examples of giving back include:

- Taking the time to say thank you to someone who has done something for you. Even if it's a delayed thank you, it's still a thank you.
- Asking people around how they are and genuinely listening to and caring about their answer.
- Spending time with friends or relatives who need your support and possibly guidance.
- Helping someone you know with a project they are working on, whether at home or at work.
- Volunteering at a school, church, or other organization.
- Donating to a good cause that you believe in.
- Helping someone out financially who is struggling at the moment.

There are many opportunities to help others and give back to the community. Make it part of your daily routine. Smile at people when you are walking down the street. Hold the door open for people. If you see someone struggling in some way, offer whatever support you can. Actively work towards being a kind human being.

Pay Attention to the Present Moment

It is quite the norm to always think about what happened in the past or worry about what will happen in the future. The problem is, we do not live in any of these places. You cannot change the past nor predict the future. What you can do is live in the present moment and try to improve your situation now. If you made mistakes in the past, learn from them, and fix them now. If you want a better future, work on improving what you can now, and it will build towards a better future. The trees that exist now were planted years ago. What you have in your life now is based on the decisions you made in the past.

It is best to live in the present moment, both physically and mentally. Pay attention to the present moment. This is called being mindful, which is something I will address more later on in this book. Being present can significantly change the way you feel about life and how you approach various challenges.

These five steps that I went over will go a long way in improving your mental well-being, which is essential to feeling good. Your mind controls your thoughts, which ultimately leads to your actions and decides your results. Take good care of your mental health.

Spiritual Well-being

Spiritual well-being acknowledges a person's quest to find a deeper meaning in life. This can be through some type of religion, but it does not have to be. When we are spiritually healthy, not only do we feel more connected to a higher power but towards other people, as well. There is more clarity when it comes to making important decisions, and the actions we take become more consistent without beliefs and values. This can be at work or in our personal lives.

Spirituality is not something that should be ignored in the pursuit of overall well-being. Once again, it does not mean you have to be religious or believe in some sort of deity. It can simply mean you believe in something greater than yourself that you cannot control.

Through spiritual well-being, we can transition from chaos to clarity through the following actions:

- Reading and reflection: You can read passages from a spiritual book or something that reaches you deep inside. Reflect on the emotions these books give you.
- Prayer: Prayer is an optional step for those who want to be connected to their faith. Prayer can help develop skills like gratitude and compassion while also putting us into a state of calmness.
- Meditation: This practice can provide us with a sense of greater self. Meditation creates space for reflection and self-awareness.
- Keep a journal: Journaling is a great way to get our emotions out in the opening without having to talk to another person about them. You can be totally honest during this practice, which can be very cathartic during the most challenging times.

Hectic days are filled with so many activities that need to be completed. Our environments are constantly buzzing, and the demands of our lifestyle make it almost impossible to get some peace. This can lead to apathy and hopelessness. If you are constantly on the move, what are you actually working towards? This is why it is even more important to obtain a sense of spiritual health. It will turn your chaotic mind into a space for clarity. Once you have clarity, you can develop a purpose.

Once your mind is clear, pause for a minute to get a bird's eye view of your life and situation. Are you currently the best version of yourself? Acknowledge all of the ways you have grown, but don't ignore the areas that still need to be improved upon. All of us have a lifetime of improvements to make. Taking these moments to reflect will give you the ability to tap into your deepest potential. It will allow you to be aware of the choices that you make and how they affect you and those around you.

All of this can help ground you and inspire you to become the person you were meant to be. Incorporate some spiritual practices into your life to improve your overall well-being.

Emotional Well-being

Emotional well-being refers to the ability to practice stress-management, be resilient, and generate positive emotions that lead to good feelings. Someone who is able to manage their emotions well under all circumstances has a high level of emotional well-being. Emotional health does not mean that you lack emotions. This just means someone is suppressing their thoughts and feelings, which is not healthy at all. A person who is willing to make themselves vulnerable and put their feelings out in the open is someone who is truly dealing with their emotional health. Emotional health also has an impact on physical health.

The following are some characteristics of an emotionally healthy person:

- Self-awareness: Self-awareness is the ability of a person to look at themselves and realize where they are in life. This includes their strengths and weaknesses, what makes them happy versus sad, their beliefs and core values, and where they ultimately want to end up in life. An emotionally healthy person is highly self-aware.
- Self-acceptance: Self-acceptance goes hand-in-hand with self-awareness. An emotionally healthy person can accept themselves for who they are and can handle adversity with more clarity, mainly because they know what they're capable of. An emotionally healthy person will realize the appropriate time to express certain emotions and may use quiet times to let all of their feelings out.
- Emotional agility: An emotionally healthy person is not immune to adversity. However, they are able to thrive during tough times because of an open mind and a curious thought process.

- Coping Skills: Coping skills are part of the toolkit for an emotionally healthy person. This means they are able to cope during the toughest times of their life. People will often build up this skill during moments of calmness to help increase their emotional capital.
- Living with purpose: Emotionally healthy people have a purpose in life that they strive for. This means they will focus on how their experiences can serve others.

As you can see, feeling good encompasses every aspect of our being. If one of these areas is off, it can eventually affect all of the others. Therefore, total and complete well-being should be our goal every day.

Chapter 2: When You Don't Feel Good

So, what happens when you don't feel good? When your physical, mental, spiritual, and emotional well-being is impacted in some way, it can create detrimental consequences in your life. There are a variety of factors that can make a person not feel good, and these must be addressed in order to improve their well-being.

Unfortunately, some of the damage has already been done because of our past. We cannot change the past, nor the impact that certain events had on our lives up to this point. What we can do is acknowledge their existence and do what we can to change things.

Factors That Affect Well-Being

There are many items in our lives, both past, and present, that personally affect our well-being in every aspect. Some of these can be controlled, while others can't. The key is to alter the things we can control and not be too impacted by the things we can't. The following are some of the factors that can negatively influence our well-being.

Adverse Childhood Experiences

Abuse, neglect, violence, drug use, and parental separation are all experiences that many children have to deal with. Unfortunately, some have to deal with many or all of them. Children who are exposed to these environments are more likely to deal with issues of not feeling good as they get older. The instability that comes from a poor household will often result in a child who engages in negative mental practices, deals with emotional irritability, and practices self-harming behavior.

Since a child cannot control their environment, a lot of damage gets done by the time they reach adulthood, and they can actually start controlling their surroundings. The bad news here is, they have no idea which direction to go in order to make changes as they were never taught to do so.

Unstable Environments

People who are living, or have lived, in unstable environments are more likely to suffer from poor well-being. This is especially true since they had less access to resources, like education or good healthcare. Also, many people from unstable environments never had the chance to develop meaningful relationships. All of these issues can lead to not feeling good from every aspect.

Social Deprivation

I spoke earlier about the importance of making genuine connections. An individual who does not have the opportunity to mix with others will eventually experience social deprivation. This phenomenon can lead to isolation and severely affect a person's well-being. Even the most introverted people among us can feel the negative effects of being isolated. Some type of human connection is needed, even if people want to be left alone for the most part.

Economic Factors

When an individual has reduced access to many resources, like money, food, education, and various opportunities for growth, they will suffer from neglect. Neglect will ultimately lead to reduced well-being in all aspects. Unfortunately, children have little to no control over their economics, which leads to many instances of not feeling good once they enter adulthood. By then, much of the damage is already done, which means there will be a lot of catching up to do.

Chronic Illnesses

Dealing with a chronic illness is never fun. Having to take medications all the time, going to various types of therapies, or having to get procedures performed just to stay alive is not an ideal situation for anybody. Chronic illnesses of any kind will put a heavy burden on someone physically, mentally, and emotionally. In addition, the person with the disease often feels like a burden to those around them, which makes them feel even worse. Imagine some of these scenarios:

- Taking dozens of medications throughout the day to help deal with various symptoms related to a disease and then having to deal with some of the effects of those medications.
- Going to dialysis treatment several times a week for many hours each day because your kidneys are no longer functioning well enough to help you survive.
- Having to go to chemotherapy treatments several times a week.
- Being in and out of the hospital constantly for various illnesses that present themselves.
- Not being able to work at your dream job because your illness precludes you from it.
- Not being able to spend quality time with family because you never know when your disease symptoms will flare-up.

Now imagine having to feel good while all of this is going on. It won't be easy for anybody.

The Impact Of Negative Well-being On Life

When we are not feeling good, it ultimately affects every area of our lives. Our circumstances will never be at peace until we learn how to make ourselves feel good in every aspect that I went over earlier. For example, if you are physically fit but mentally exhausted, then you will still deal with many issues that will bring you down. The goal is to find balance in all of these areas by engaging in the many activities that were discussed in chapter one. We will learn now why it is important by going over the negative impact that poor well-being has on all of us.

The Impact On Work

The health and wellness of a person have a major impact on their work performance, productivity, employee retention, and a company's bottom line. Employees with poor well-being have lower work output. During a major international study done by the O.C. Tanner Institute, of the 2,363 employees who were surveyed, the majority of them reported only a 64% maximum output when they weren't feeling well in some way. Employees and workers in this position are also less likely to be collaborative and will have negative views about working in teams.

When an individual is in poor physical health, they have reduced energy, sustainability, and focus. This makes it more difficult to put in work during all of the necessary work hours, and important tasks either get done half-hazard or get ignored completely. The same holds true for some dealing with a lack of mental, spiritual, or emotional well-being. All of these areas make it nearly impossible to do your best work on the job. As a result, promotions and other opportunities will pass you by. Even worse, you may soon be without a job. This is why it's important to take care of your well-being anytime you can, so you feel good most of the time.

In turn, issues at work can also lead to poor well-being. It is in a business's best interest to have employees who are healthy in every way possible. Otherwise, they lose money with poor performance, sick calls, and low productivity. While a company or organization cannot make a person healthy, they can certainly look out for problems that are creating a poor work environment.

A company can, and its administration can do their best to make sure they are prepared for crisis situations. They can be proactive instead of reactive. They can be aware of their employees' needs and assess whether any of them are being overworked. A company cannot demand that its employees work nonstop and then expect top-notch results on a continuous basis. Finally, a business can ensure a positive work environment so their workers are not stricken with mental anguish. The worst thing to have within an organization are employees that do not want to be there.

Employee health programs can be beneficial, as well. Promoting health through onsite wellness checkups, allowing employees to work fewer hours in a week, and even adapting an exercise program on location can help increase employee satisfaction and overall well-being.

In addition to poor health and well-being affecting work, work can also negatively affect your well-being. All of us would love to go to work, perform our duties, and leave to enjoy the rest of the day. Unfortunately, it does not always work out this way. While a job can provide security, nurture a sense of purpose, and feed professional hunger, the wrong job can be toxic in so many ways:

- Many workers struggle to balance their lives because they feel they always have to be available for work. This can cause unnecessary strain on themselves and their relationships. It's one thing to love your job, but it's another thing to make it your life. It does not have to be this way.
- Rotational shiftwork is a common occurrence in certain industries. This means that employees do not work the same shifts every day. This can significantly disrupt the body clock and throw off someone's sleep cycle.
- No breaks: When the work keeps piling up, and you have no idea how to finish all of it, the last thing on your mind will be to step away and take a break. Eventually, you will experience lethargy, stiff muscles, and a reduced mood. To combat this makes sure to take scheduled breaks where you actually step away from your desk.

- With strange work hours, abnormal eating habits can become common, as well. Instead of eating a healthy meal during the day, many workers opt for quick snacks from the vending machine or going by the drive-thru really quickly.
- The commute to and from work can be very taxing, especially if you are traveling during rush-hour. Some mindful techniques that I will go over later on, can be helpful in these situations.
- Positive company culture is critical for the well-being of the employees, but this is not always the case. There are many toxic work environments that are created by either the management, workers, or both.

If you notice these factors affecting you at work and reducing your overall well-being, then it's time to take the issues to management. If that doesn't solve the problem, you may need to find a new work environment. Unfortunately, our work environments are often negative and cause us great mental and emotional harm.

The Impact On Relationships

When we are not in a positive state of well-being, our relationships are also affected. We tend to always think about things in the negative, including anything associated with our partners. Rather than enjoying the good things about our relationships, our minds automatically revert to all of the things going wrong. This results in being fixated on the bad things, and the relationship can never be happy if this is the case.

This is not exclusive to relationships with our partners. Even connections with family members, friends, coworkers, neighbors, and anyone else close to us can be severed. By being in a negative state of well-being or not feeling good, your partner's good qualities will never get to shine through as all of their negative qualities will be magnified. Yes, all of us have unappealing traits about us, but if we only focus on those, all of the great things about our relationships will fall through the cracks.

Not feeling good will result in abusive relationships of all kinds. As a result, neither member will be happy in their roles. Having negative feelings can result in never forgetting the sins of the past. This means that if your partner did something years ago that may not even be relevant now, it can still be stuck in your mind and impact how you treat the relationship. In addition, anything negative about your past that's not even related to the current relationship can have a negative effect. Forgiveness for anything becomes a thing of the past, and every wrongdoing that occurs is another hit that slowly breaks the relationships apart.

By living in a negative state of well-being, you will never support anyone's dreams, even those who are closest to you. Instead, you will always ridicule others and put them down. In turn, they will do the same to you, which creates even more damage. Supporting each other is essential to any relationship to keep it healthy. If you don't take care of yourself and feel good, you will not be able to provide long-term support to anyone else. Eventually, they will also stop providing support for you.

When you don't feel good, it is very difficult to maintain positive relationships. Even if individuals stay together, there will never be true happiness, and everyone will live in complete misery. As you can see, when you don't feel good, other people around you can be affected too. While we all have our days where we don't feel right, no matter how good things are, when it becomes a chronic issue, that's when major relationship problems occur.

The Impact On Health

Being in a negative state of well-being can be the result of poor health. In addition, poor health can also be the result of negative well-being or not feeling good. There is an obvious connection between emotional and mental health. When we are not feeling good, these areas of our lives can be impacted negatively too. For example, not feeling good can lead to:

- Chronic sadness and eventually depression
- Anger issues
- Self-harming practices
- An inability to focus or reduced mental clarity
- Anxiety

However, it is not just limited to this. Our physical health can also be impacted. When our well-being is not good, our thoughts shift towards the negative. While this initial moment of not feeling good can be the result of poor health, it can also lead to poor health and become a vicious cycle. Negativity can manifest itself in many ways, including:

- Cynicism: Having a general distrust of people and what they are about. While it's okay to put your guard up a little bit, you must have some faith that people have good intentions if you want to keep moving forward and not always be in a negative state of mind.
- Hostility: Always being unfriendly towards other people. Hostile people have a hard time developing relationships, which can be very unhealthy.
- Filtering: Only noticing the bad things in a situation and taking out all of the bad stuff.
- Polarized Thinking: This is the belief that people cannot have flaws. They are either perfect in every way or horrible human beings.
- Catastrophizing: Believing that a disastrous situation is always looming.
- Emotional Reasoning: Using emotions to define what is real, instead of using logic.
- Fallacy of change: Believing that if circumstances change, you will become happy. For example, once you get past a certain event or find a new

job, happiness will come. But true happiness is a state of mind and not dependent on the situation.
- Blaming: Holding other people responsible for anything that goes wrong in your life and feeling like you are always the victim.

Many of these manifestations can result in poor relationships too, which I discussed in the earlier section. No matter how negativity is outwardly displayed, it can have harmful effects on the body. Negativity leads to the stress response, which is needed for survival in certain situations. However, during stress, a hormone called cortisol is released into the bloodstream, which creates certain physiological changes to make us more alert and focused.

Long-term negativity, or being in a poor state of well-being for an extended period of time, will slow down digestion, decrease immune system function, lead to heart disease, increase the chance for diabetes, and even put you at a higher risk for certain cancers. When you constantly don't feel good in this regard, you can end up with the following symptoms:

- Headache
- Chest pain
- Fatigue
- Upset stomach
- Sleep problems
- Anxiety

- Depression
- Social withdrawal
- Poor eating practices

Picture having to live with these symptoms on a daily basis. How much of a strain would that put on your life? Well, many people who don't feel good are dealing with these issues every day, which will result in never living a happy life. As you continue to be unhappy, more chronic sickness will come your way. Have you ever noticed that those who are always happy become sick a lot less? It is not just because they handle it better. Our physiology is literally different when we are feeling good, and this results in fewer sick days.

The bottom line here is that not feeling good will have a negative effect on many areas of our lives. How we feel on the inside and the way we view the world play a significant role in how various aspects of our lives turn out. This is why feeling good therapy is so important.

Chapter 3: Negative Emotions And Disorders

Every person you run into in this world is fighting battles that you cannot see. The person standing next to you in line may have just lost their job. The individual who is driving next to you on the highway may have a child who is sick. The person serving you at the bank could be dealing with many mental health issues and is near a mental breakdown. Even you are fighting your own battles and how other people treat, you can make all the difference in the world.

So far, in this book, we have discussed the idea of poor well-being and not feeling good from the standpoint of not taking care of one's self. However, there are many mood disorders that exist which cause people to behave erratically and not respond in the same manner as most people would. The focus of this chapter will be to discuss specific negative emotions and mental health disorders and how they can impact our well-being. Many of these illnesses have similar traits, while others are completely in their own bubble. Still, you may notice a lot of crossover between all of them.

Negative Emotions

Depression

Depression is a major mood disorder that affects millions of people around the world. It affects how you think, feel, and act. Many people do not understand this illness, and if you are not going through it, it is exceedingly difficult to describe to anyone. Depression leads to feelings of sadness and loss of interest in activities you once enjoyed. It is not a feeling that someone can just get over. It goes well beyond general sadness and can lead to conditions of extreme sorrow. Telling a person to just get over their depression can make their situation much worse. Symptoms of chronic depression include:

- Feeling sad or having a depressed mood, often for no obvious reason.
- A loss of interest in activities that were once enjoyed.
- Change in appetite which leads to either weight loss or weight gain. Either way, people are developing poor eating habits.
- Trouble sleeping well or sleeping too much.
- Lethargy or fatigue. An overall loss of energy.
- Increase in purposeful movements, like pacing, rocking back-and-forth in a chair, clicking a pen, or handwringing.
- Slowed movement or speech that is very noticeable. This is when you see people walking slow and being unusually slow to respond.
- Feeling worthless or guilty for no reason. They feel like everything is their fault.
- Difficulty in concentrating, thinking, or decision-making.
- Thoughts of death, suicide, or self-harm.

Clinical depression has to be diagnosed by a medical professional. The symptoms have to last at least two weeks and must represent a major change from the previous level of functioning. This is because other medical issues, like thyroid problems, neurological issues, or nutrient deficiency, can lead to similar symptoms as depression. It is important to rule those out first before coming to a conclusive diagnosis.

A major loss or negative event can cause anyone to spiral into a state of depression. However, these feelings have an explanation in this regard and are usually short-lived. With chronic depression, there might be no explanation for why a person is feeling morose, and the emotions can just come out of nowhere. In fact, everything can be going perfectly in someone's life, and they will still deal with issues of depression.

So, sadness is not the same as depression. The grieving process that comes from loss or pain is natural and should not be confused with a mental health disorder. Of course, a person with depression could react completely different to loss, as well. People who are experiencing loss often describe themselves as being depressed, but this is not completely accurate. The emotions and thoughts may be similar to a degree, but there are significant differences to look out for:

- When a person is grieving from a loss, their feelings come in waves, changing from positive to negative. This means they will be extremely sad one minute about losing someone and then become happy when they start thinking about fond memories. A person who is depressed will have a constantly decreased mood that lasts several weeks.

- With grief, a person does not lose confidence in themselves, generally. Their sadness is only directed at the loss they suffered. A person who is depressed will often feel useless and spend their time self-loathing.
- With grief, thoughts of death may occur in extreme moments when the person is thinking about reuniting with their loved ones, but these thoughts usually dissipate fairly quickly. With depression, thoughts of suicide exist because a person feels worthless and does not believe they bring any value to the world.

In certain cases, an individual who is going through difficult moments in their life, like a loss of a loved one or being a victim of assault, can become depressed. When grief and depression coexist, the symptoms are much more severe. It is important to distinguish between grief and sadness versus chronic depression in terms of getting the necessary help.

Risk Factors For Depression

There are many causes out there for depression. Even when a person is living in ideal circumstances, they can still be suffering from this debilitating mood disorder. A person who appears happy on the outside may not be feeling good on the inside. They just don't want to burden anyone else with their problems. Some factors leading to depression are:

- Biochemistry: The chemistry of a person's brain can contribute to depression.
- Genetics: This illness can run in the family. It can be passed down from generation to generation, and many times, identical twins, even when separated at birth, can both be dealing with symptoms of chronic depression.
- Personality: The personality of an individual plays a big role too. People with low self-esteem, who are easily overwhelmed by the stresses in the world, are more likely to experience depression. Look out for pessimistic behavior in this regard.
- Environmental factors: Your surroundings can also lead to depression. Continuous exposure to violence, abuse, neglect, or poverty can make certain people more vulnerable to depression.

If you feel that you are suffering from depression, it is important to get the help you need. It might be the reason you are generally not feeling good.

Anxiety

Everyone goes through short-term anxiety at certain points in their lives. Worried about a test the next day, being apprehensive about starting a new job, or getting nervous when meeting new people are all normal emotions that people go through. Occasional anxiety is usually nothing to worry about. In fact, it can increase your performance by making you more alert and prepared. When anxiety becomes chronic and debilitating, that's when it is an issue. People who suffer from anxiety disorders frequently have intense and persistent moments of worry and fear about everyday situations. They wake up each morning and are terrified about going to work, even though they go to the same job every day. Even though they hang out with the same group of people, they never feel completely comfortable. They are always on edge for some reason.

At some point, these feelings of anxiety can become debilitating and interfere with daily activities. Emotions become difficult to control, and panic attacks become common. People with anxiety will start to avoid places or situations that bring them anxiety to prevent these feelings from occurring. Eventually, the symptoms will grow worse and continue seeping into all areas of life. Soon enough, anxiety issues will become completely unavoidable. Many of these symptoms of this illness start in childhood and grow throughout the adult years, especially if they are not addressed appropriately. Some of the common signs and symptoms are:

- Feeling tense, nervous, and restless. They are always on edge but don't know why.
- Have a sense of impending danger, panic, or doom, even if there is no reason for it.

- Rapid breathing or hyperventilation.
- Trembling, sweating, or grinding teeth.
- Feeling very weak and tired.
- Trouble concentrating or thinking about anything else but their present worry.
- Having difficulty sleeping.
- Experiencing digestive problems.
- Unable to control their worry. They always believe something is about to go wrong.
- Trying to avoid things that trigger their anxiety.

Anxiety can also be categorized into different types of disorders:

- Agoraphobia: Is when you have a fear of wide-open spaces. You avoid places purposefully that will bring you anxiety.
- Claustrophobia: This, on the other hand, is a fear of closed-off spaces. For example, being in an elevator or crowded room. The new health concern plaguing the world has created an issue where certain people are unable to wear masks for long periods of time due to claustrophobia.
- Generalized Anxiety Disorder: Includes persistent and excessive anxiety about activities and events. Even routine activities that a person does all the time can create anxiety, and the worry is out of proportion to the actual circumstance. For

example, a person breaks into a sweat when it is their turn to order food at a restaurant.

- Panic Disorder: Involves sudden feelings of intense anxiety that are repeated episodes and reach their peak within minutes. These peaks are called panic attacks. A person going through these will have feelings of impending doom, rapid breathing, fast heart rate, and diaphoresis. Similar symptoms can occur during a fight-or-flight response, but this panic attack is under unusual circumstances.
- Separation Anxiety Disorder: This is a childhood disorder characterized by excessive anxiety that is unusual for a child's development level. It is related to the separation of a child from their parents or other influential adults.
- Social Anxiety Disorder: This involves high levels of anxiety, fear, and avoidance of most social situations due to feelings of embarrassment, self-consciousness, and fear of being judged.

There are many other specific anxiety disorders that can pop up at any moment or situation in a person's life. Basically, anxiety goes well beyond regular fear because the emotions are completely out of line with the actual situation. While a person without anxiety may be fearful during that moment, someone with anxiety could completely fall apart.

Causes Of Anxiety

The causes of anxiety disorder are not fully understood and may be linked to some underlying health issues. Chronic illnesses can be lead to anxiety, and anxiety can also be one of the earlier indicators of a health issue. Examples of medical problems that have a link to anxiety include:

- Heart disease
- Diabetes
- Thyroid issues
- Respiratory disorders like asthma
- Drug misuse
- Chronic pain
- Digestive problems

Anxiety can also be a side effect of certain medications. The factors that make it more likely that your anxiety is due to a medical condition are:

- No familial history of anxiety disorder.
- Absences of anxiety disorder as a youth.
- You don't avoid certain situations or people because of your anxiety.
- You have a sudden bout of anxiety that is not related to an event, but you have no previous history of anxiety.

Some risk factors for anxiety include:

- Trauma: People who witnessed abuse and trauma or endured it themselves are at a higher risk of developing an anxiety disorder at some point in their lives. This is especially true for children.
- Stress due to illness: Health conditions can cause serious concerns about things like treatment plans, finances, and what the future holds.
- Stress buildup: When many things are causing stress, and it is all piling up, it can trigger excessive anxiety.
- Personality: Certain personality types are more prone to getting anxiety.
- Other mental health disorders: People who suffer from other mental health disorders, like the aforementioned depression, are at a higher risk for anxiety, as well.
- Genetics: Having blood relatives with anxiety disorders will increase the chance of you having it.
- Drugs or alcohol: The misuse of drugs or alcohol, as well as withdrawals, can lead to a worsening of anxiety and even cause it.

Post-Traumatic Stress Disorder

Post-traumatic stress disorder, or PTSD, is a mental health disorder that gets triggered by some sort of terrifying or traumatic event. The event can be either personal or something they witnessed. We mostly associate PTSD with those who served in the military; but other professions, like police officers, first responders, or anyone else who experienced a traumatic event in some way, can become a victim of this disorder. For example, an assault victim or someone who watched a loved one pass away can suffer from PTSD.

PTSD is marked by nightmares, flashbacks, severe anxiety, and uncontrollable thoughts. Most people who go through a traumatic event will have some difficulty adjusting and coping in the short-term. With time and good self-care, the issues related to the event slowly subside. With PTSD, the symptoms continually get worse and can last for months or even years.

PTSD symptoms can actually be grouped into four different types and can vary greatly from person to person:

Inclusive

- Recurring and unwanted memories of the distressing event.
- Having flashbacks or reliving the events as if they are happening again in real-time.

- Recurring nightmares about the traumatic events.
- Severe distress or specific physical reactions that remind the person about the traumatic event.

Avoidance

- Avoiding thinking or talking about the traumatic event.
- Avoiding any places, people, activities, or situations that are reminders of the event.

Negative Changes in Thinking and Mood

- Constant negative thoughts about self, other people, or the rest of the world.
- Having no hope for the future.
- Memory problems related to the event, including remembering key aspects of it.
- Difficulty in developing and maintaining close relationships.
- Having a lack of interest in things you once enjoyed.
- Having a hard time experiencing any positive emotions.

Changes in Physical and Emotional Reactions

- Getting frightened or startled fairly quickly.

- Never letting your guard down. Always believing that possible danger exists.
- Excessive drinking, drug use, and other self-destructive behaviors.
- Difficulty sleeping and concentrating.
- Erratic behavior and angry outbursts.

The intensity of PTSD can vary over time. The symptoms can become worse during times of great stress, and when certain events serve as reminders of the past. If the symptoms you are having are severe, lasting over a month, or causing majors issues in your life, it may be time to see a doctor or a licensed therapist.

Low Self-Esteem

Low self-esteem is when a person does not have a high opinion of themselves in regard to their abilities and capabilities. In many cases, they feel like less of a person than other people and feel they bring no real value to the world. Self-esteem does not mean humility. It has long-term damaging effects, like not speaking up when you want something, or not going after a goal because you think you don't deserve it. Eventually, low self-esteem can lead to relationship problems, issues at work, poor health, and damaging behavior. All of these will result in poor well-being and a person not feeling good. It is important to understand the signs of low self-esteem:

- Difficulty speaking up about what you want and prioritizing your own needs and desires.
- Saying sorry for everything, even if it's not your fault. It gets to the point where you are sorry for just existing. You feel guilty for taking up space.
- Never rocking the boat. While you should not purposefully try to upset people, sometimes, it is a byproduct of demanding what you want in life. Instead, people with low self-esteem always follow the crown, whether they want to or not.
- Not feeling deserving or capable of having more. This can lead to never obtaining desired goals, being stuck in toxic relationships, and having low standards for everything. It feels good to win, and when your self-esteem is low, you will never feel like a winner.
- Have difficulty making choices and then standing by them. You will be easily swayed.
- Having a negative self-perception. People with low self-esteem believe others will never like or accept them. They will often go out of their way to become likable, even if it's to their own detriment.
- Have a critical and/or abusive internal dialogue. It is one thing to make assessments and see where you can improve. It is a totally different thing to speak harshly and put yourself down.

In order to feel good and have a strong sense of well-being, you need to improve your self-esteem. When you do, you will have higher satisfaction with yourself. You will care less about what others think and worry more about your own opinion of yourself. The following are some ways to build your self-esteem:

- Prioritize exercise that feels good to you. Even small amounts of movement are helpful. Exercise can boost your serotonin and other feel-good hormones in your body, which will help you feel calmer, stronger, and in better control.
- Put your own needs before anyone else's. This is not selfish; it is a necessity. If you don't take care of yourself, soon enough, you will not be able to take care of anyone else.
- Make a list of your priorities and goals in life. Make it a habit to outline your goals each day. Do not let other people's needs derail what you have planned for your life.
- Do not automatically say "yes" to everything. You are not obligated to be at everyone's beck-and-call all the time. Before committing to something, pause for a moment and seek out the reason for doing this. Is it something you want to do, or are you just trying to get someone's approval?

- Use techniques to start lifting yourself up. Leave yourself positive messages and love notes in random places. This includes your home, office, and car.
- Start telling yourself some positive affirmations. You can make up your own or get some from the internet. Apps such as ThinkUp and Shine are great places to get positive affirmations.
- Notice when you are comparing yourself to others and try to eliminate this practice. You will have your own unique qualities that make you special, so don't believe that another person's gifts are somehow impeding on your value. One way to avoid comparing yourself to others is by avoiding social media.
- Find ways to relax, unwind, and pamper yourself. Don't be afraid to invest in yourself because that is the best investment you can make.
- Eliminate the phrase "I'm sorry" from your vocabulary unless you are actually apologizing for something you did. Instead, use phrases like "Excuse me" or "I beg your pardon," whenever appropriate.
- If needed, seek out professional help.

Pessimism

Pessimism is when your mind automatically reverts to the negative aspects of any situation. You never see the positive or potential results because you are overly focused on what could go wrong instead. There are always storm clouds looming in the distance, and the glass is never half full. Basically, pessimism leads to expecting the worst out of any situation, even if things are going well. It is one thing to be prepared for the worst; it is another to just expect the worst. This is a poor mindset to have and can lead to many issues with mental health. Also, it will prevent you from living the life you want because you are worried that things won't turn out well anyway.

Eventually, pessimism can lead to feelings of isolation, anxiety, sleep disorders, resentment, and hostility. If you are a pessimistic person, then you need to be able to handle it. To do this, you must have realistic expectations, rather than extreme positive or negative positions. This is the recipe for good health and balance in life.

Mild amounts of pessimism actually have some positive benefits. Mainly, it keeps a person alert and aware of their surroundings. It can be a protective mechanism against some dangerous situations or people. Basically, mild pessimism promotes a healthy level of skepticism. The key is to not let it get so out of hand that you never trust or believe in anything.

As you can see, when you are dealing with negative emotions and mental health disorders, your overall well-being is affected greatly. As a result, you will never be able to feel good about anything. In further chapters, I will discuss more about overcoming these issues that impact how we feel.

Why Kindness Is Important

I want to end this chapter by explaining why kindness is so beneficial. We literally do not know what people are dealing with every day, and I think that point has been proven with what we have already gone over in this book. Whether someone is suffering from a mental health disorder or not, they are still facing challenges that can knock them down at any moment. You being a kind person to them might be the one thing that holds them up and keeps them moving forward. The power of kindness impacts your life and others.

Kindness Makes You Happy

Acting kindly to others will help you relax and feel good about yourself. Have you ever noticed how you feel when you treat someone poorly? Well, if you are like most people, you feel pretty awful in every way. The next time you slip and treat someone bad in any way, whether it's through words or actions, stop for a moment and notice how you feel. Chances are, you will not feel good at all.

When you are kind, you will feel very good. Kindness to others can take you out of sadness and actually make you a happy person. Here are some examples of kindness creating happiness:

- When we smile at someone as they walk by and they smile back, you feel good at that moment.
- When we buy someone else a gift, instead of getting something for ourselves, they love it, and we are happier giving rather than receiving. Remember the old saying that it is better to give than to receive. That saying is not just relevant during Christmas time.
- When someone drops their items, and you help pick them up, you feel good knowing you were able to help someone.

Small acts of kindness towards others can make you feel good about yourself, and this creates happiness.

Fewer Negative Emotions

As you display kindness to others, there will be far more positive emotions, which will leave less room for negative emotions. When you are kind, you will feel less stressed. Being a mean person is actually very stressful. You hold onto a lot of tension, which can lead to anger, sadness, and fear. When you are nice to others, much of this tension goes away, and so do many of the negative emotions.

Kindness Is Contagious

Just like a cold, if you stand around people long enough and show kindness, they will eventually become kind too. This is not a guarantee, but it happens in many cases. People are drawn to those who are kind individuals and look for this attribute in friends and partners. Kindness is a prosocial behavior that leads to acceptance and popularity. This was apparent in many school settings. The person who was often the most likable was also the friendliest.

When you are kind to people, it goes well beyond just your realm. It spreads like wildfire. The people around you glean from your kindness, and they go around and spread it to other people. Kindness is contagious, and you can influence the world by using it.

Kindness has many positive results for anyone lucky enough to be around it. Being nice puts you in a better state of mind, and it helps other people feel better too. You don't have to engage in any grandiose activity to show kindness to others. It can be simple acts done on a regular basis. These are the things that people remember the most. Some examples include:

- Holding the door open for someone.
- Sharing your lunch with a friend who forgot there's.
- Randomly smiling at a stranger.

- Offering to help out on a project, even if you have no responsibility for it.
- Telling someone you are close to how you feel about them.
- When someone does something well, compliment them, regardless of how big or small it was.
- Don't kick someone while they are down. If you cannot help someone, at least stay out of their way and don't make things any worse.

Kindness will go much farther than you think, even if you can't see the results in real-time. This will be the starting point of starting to feel good.

Chapter 4: Shifting The Mindset

I have mentioned the idea of mindset and the role it plays in developing our thoughts and actions, which ultimately leads to results. Almost any successful person you talk to in any field will tell you that their mindset is what helped them make the necessary adjustments to start creating the life they imagined. The focus of this chapter will be the importance of mindset and how shifting it towards the positive can drastically change our circumstances.

What Is The Mindset

Your mindset will dictate how you view yourself and the world around you. It can make you believe that your potential is limitless or that you are destined to only reach a particular position in life. If an individual believes that he will be a successful business owner someday, then his chances of becoming so increases because he is planting the thought in his mind. He will most likely get farther than someone who believes he could never achieve this feat.

There are two types of mindsets: The fixed mindset and the growth mindset. These different types are often developed at a young age and depend on the type of environment a child grows up in. The fixed mindset is when someone believes their abilities in life are innate, and there is nothing that can be done to change them. Those with a fixed mindset believe that failure occurs because there is something lacking within themselves.

People with a growth mindset don't believe they are born with everything they have. They feel that they can learn anything or acquire any ability they need to succeed at what they want. Basically, they know they can improve and become the people they want to be, rather than just being stuck where they are. They don't let setbacks stop them.

The environment and outside influences play a significant role in how a mindset is developed. Specific messages you receive from influential people in your life, like parents, teachers, friends, or mentors, can form your mindset for the better or worse. Children who are told that they are not smart enough for something and will never achieve it will likely develop a fixed mindset. On the other hand, children who are encouraged to improve on things they are not good at are more likely to develop a growth mindset.

Children with a fixed mindset will grow up to be adults who put limitations on themselves. They will constantly take the safe route and never challenge themselves. Therefore, they will never grow to become more well-rounded people. This will cause the world to pass them by as they sit in their bubble being comfortable, and never taking any chances.

Someone who has a fixed mindset will view setbacks and failures as a sings that they are not good enough and never will be. Someone with a growth mindset will see setbacks and failures as a learning opportunity. They don't just accept the fact they are not good enough. They become good enough through hard work and sacrifice. The good news here is that you are not stuck with your mindset. You can change it, even as an adult. So, if you have always lived with limitations using a fixed mindset approach, then you need to start adjusting towards a growth mindset.

Your mindset will affect every area of your life, including career, health, relationships, and other personal life issues. This is why it's important to adopt the right thought processes. You will never change and prosper for the better unless you do.

Consider these two stories:

Mike has just been let go from his job at a major corporation. It was a job he enjoyed and thought he was good at. After losing his position, Mike decides he was not good enough for it anyway and starts looking for a lower-level position. He does not believe he has the capability of doing his previous job well for any other company.

James has been let-go from his job at a major corporation. He loved the job and was surprised he lost it because he thought he was doing a good job. Instead of wondering why he lost it, James decides there are better opportunities out there, begins fixing and updating his resume, and applies for many higher positions. Eventually, he gets hired into a company, and his new job pays more than what he was making before.

As you can see, having two separate mindsets, even when the situations are similar, can make a huge difference. Let's start working on ways to shift your mindset, so you live a better life and start feeling good too.

Shifting Your Mindset

Imagine thinking and believing that your potential is limitless. You have the ability to accomplish great things in this world. The growth mindset is exactly what it sounds like: you believe you always have the capability to grow and become a different person. The way you were born or the way you grew up does not have to be who you are for the remainder of your life. The basic qualities you have can be cultivated through effort.

This is an important mindset to have because it changes the way you view yourself and your surroundings. People throughout history who have succeeded at the highest level are those who developed a growth mindset at some point in their lives. With this mindset, the hand you are dealt with is just the starting point of where you can ultimately go. Some people are born in huts with no prospects and end up becoming world-renowned figures. Others are born on third base and end up losing everything. The key factor here is their mindsets. The person born in a hut believed there was a better world out there, and the individual born on third base thought his destiny was set.

I will go over some specific techniques to help you start shifting your mindset towards growth. Start becoming the person you were meant to be and not what the world tells you to be.

- Acknowledge embrace imperfections. If you always hide your weaknesses, you will never overcome them.
- Do not view challenges as stopping points, but as opportunities to become better. Having a growth mindset means you relish opportunities for self-improvement. The only way for this to occur is to be challenged in some way.
- Try different learning tactics. What works for some people will not necessarily work for others. There is a great meme out there in the world that

shows various animals standing in a group. The instructor asks all of them to climb a tree. Of course, the monkey is excited, while the elephant, fish, and other animals are frustrated or confused. Just because you don't have the same skills as others does not mean you are not talented.

- Never believe that your brain is fixed. In fact, it is constantly being remolded with all of the new information you are taking in.
- Replace the word "failing" with "learning." Every failure is an opportunity to learn. As long as you learn, it won't be wasted.
- Stop seeking the approval of others. Honestly, what other people think about your life is none of your concern. If you constantly wait for others' approval, you are sacrificing your own potential for growth.
- Value the process over the end result. The process of getting to your goal is important because that is where all of the learning takes place. If you are just focused on Points A and B, you will miss out on everything that happened in between. You will have successes and failures along the way, and you can learn from both to help you in the future.
- Celebrate growth with other people without rubbing it in. Celebrate their growth and yours alike.

- Emphasize growth over speed. Life is not a race, and as long as you are growing continuously, that is good enough.
- Reward actions instead of traits. Instead of just seeing yourself as smart, reward yourself for actions that are smart. For example, reading every day, learning new skills, waking up early, and exercising daily are all smart activities.
- Place effort ahead of talent. The hard work you put in should be praised more highly than specific skills.
- Learn from other people's mistakes. You don't have the time to experience all of the mistakes the world has to offer. Therefore, when someone else has an experience, learn from it, as well.
- Every time you accomplish a goal, make another goal so you can keep moving.
- Don't try to save face all the time. Start taking risks and be willing to screw up, even if people are watching you. This will make it easier to take risks in the future.
- It takes time to learn things. Don't expect to master every topic under the sun in a single sitting.
- Take extreme ownership of your attitude. Once you develop a growth mindset, it is time to start recognizing and owning it. Be proud of it, and let it guide you through your life and career.

How To Level Up Your Mindset

Your mindset is essentially your belief system, and it will ultimately set up everything that comes to you in your life. In order to achieve your desired goals, your mindset has to level up to your aspirations. You can want all of the greatest things in the world, but if you do not believe you can achieve them, then it's futile. Your limiting mindset is holding you back from great things, and it's time to officially make an upgrade with the following techniques.

Change Your Self-Talk

The way you talk to yourself is a direct reflection of your mindset. If you are telling yourself things like, "I am not good enough," or "I will never be able to accomplish that," then you have already lost. You may as well not even continue. So, before you go any further, start changing your self-talk. Start telling yourself things like, "I have the ability to do this, and I will figure out how!" Your thought will create your actions, your actions will create your results, and your results will create your reality. It is a pretty appealing pattern if you allow it to play out this way. Start changing your self-talk to something more empowering. It might sound a little cliched, but it really does work.

Change You Language

Once you have changed your inner dialogue with positive self-talk, the next action is to change the way you talk to other people. You need to stop complaining about your problems because, first of all, people stop caring after a while, if they did at all in the first place, and second, your complaints will be all that you focus on. Instead, start telling people about the good things n your life. This does not have to be done in a braggadocious way. Just bring up what's going well whenever it comes up in casual conversation. By doing this, your mind will remain focused on positive things, as well.

Determine The Mindset You Need And Then Act Accordingly

After picking a goal, you want to achieve, determine the mindset you need to get there. Research other individuals who have obtained the goals you are after and determine what type of mindset they had and mimic them. For instance, people who are healthy and fit love taking care of their bodies, always get a workout in, pay attention to the food they eat and monitor their habits. Most of all, they believe they can achieve their fitness goals when they put their mind to it. If you want to be fit like them, you must follow their same mindset for success. Even before you achieve your goal, act as if you already have the thought process of someone who is there, and you will effectively trick your brain into adopting a new mindset, which you will follow up with action.

Learn And Apply

Once again, the best way to become a successful person is to copy the strategies of other successful people and make adjustments as needed. Read books about some of the greatest minds of the past, attend seminars put on by successful people in their fields, and learn from mindset experts through various online courses.

Surround Yourself With The Right People

You need to start changing your inner circle. If you constantly spend time with people who are buzzkills and always put down your dreams, then you will be stuck in mediocrity. Instead, start hanging around other successful people who have adopted winning mindsets. You will be able to glean from them and start shifting your mindset in positive ways, as well. Learn how successful people think by surrounding yourself with them and match their mindsets.

Create New Habits To Support your Mindset

As you develop your new mindset, you must also incorporate habits that reinforce it; if you are adjusting from a "fixed" to "growth" mindset, schedule time in your day for learning opportunities, like reading. A mindset is a way of thinking, and habits are the building blocks that help support it. For example, if you develop a mindset of improving your business, you can take daily actions that will result in improving your business.

Get Out Of Your Comfort Zone

Nothing was ever accomplished inside of a comfort zone. You need to put yourself in challenging situations that will give you no other option but to rise above and upgrade your mindset. The idea here is to engineer an environment to train your brain.

When you start changing your mindset, that is when you start feeling good in life. Will everything be perfect? No, definitely not. However, we are after good here and not perfection. In order to be in a positive state of wellbeing, you must have the belief that you can be.

Embrace Change Through A new Mindset

In order to feel god in our lives, we must be able to embrace change. Change is inevitable, and if we do not accept, we will simply get left behind. This is a major hurdle that many people face, and that is why many of them suffer. By trying to keep things the same, you are fighting a battle, you cannot win. Yes, change is scary, and it comes at you fast. You can train your brain to better handle change through various mental exercises. These trainings are not always pleasant, but they are effective, so give them a try.

Retrain Your Brain By Noticing Three Positive Changes Per Day

Look around on a daily basis and try to notice at least three changes that have occurred throughout history that have made the world a better place and improved people's ability to live life. For example, sending emails in lieu of snail mail has made communication much faster and more convenient. The smartphone has given us the ability to communicate with people all over the world. The refrigerator has made it possible to keep food longer without it becoming spoiled. Notice these types of changes in your surroundings every day, and you will slowly realize that change can be a great thing.

Write Your Own Post-Mortem

I don't mean to get dark here, but I want you to think about your life and where things would be either one year, five years, or ten years down the line if everything remained stagnant. Think about what other people might be doing to get ahead in their lives and how you can be left behind if you don't change in a similar manner. For example, are people at work coming up with innovative ways to complete projects that make everything more efficient? During your post-mortem, write down everything you can think of about how your life will suffer if you refuse to make changes.

Focus On your Long-Term Vision

Always keep your long-term goals and the vision that comes with them in your mind. Even though change is necessary, it is not always pleasant. You will go through some dark moments, and in order to get through these, you must be able to look beyond your present conditions and see what you can accomplish.

Accept That Change Will Happen No Matter What

Whether you are ready or not, change is going to happen, and if you don't jump on that bandwagon, you will be left behind. If that is your goal, by all means, avoid change. However, the world is going to be a different place years down the line, and it will happen with or without you. So, stop getting in your own way and begin embracing change.

Eliminate The "Sunk-Costs" Mindset

Basically, the more time you have invested into something, the less likely you are to part with it. Even if not letting go is harming you in the end, it is still hard to not stay attached. Don't let the fear of losing what you've already invested in guide your decision-making. You must always be looking for ways to improve your life, and if something is holding you back, even if you've invested in it heavily, you must release the grip to keep moving forward.

Developing A New Habit

A major part of shifting your mindset, which we have mentioned already, is to develop new habits to support your new thoughts. Habits are tendencies that are ingrained in us, sometimes from birth. As a result, they can be difficult to change, especially when shifting from a bad habit to a good habit. In this final section of the chapter, I will go over some general steps on how to create a habit that you can start using right away.

Focus On One New Habit

If we try to change too many of our habits all at once, we will spread our willpower out too thin. For this reason, we must focus on changing one habit at a time. That way, our willpower can be channeled into one area for maximum effort. Identify which habit is most pressing and focus your energy on changing it. For example, you might have a bad habit of waking up at the very last minute every morning, and you want to change this habit. A goal in this regard can be to wake up an hour earlier than you already are, so you can take care of some tasks in the morning.

Commit To Thirty Days

There are many theories discussing how long it takes to actually develop a new habit. The consensus from many people is that it takes at least 21 days. Basically, you must perform your new routine for 21 days straight before it can become a habit and done automatically. I will go a little further and tell you to give yourself at least 30 days. The length of time can vary from person to person but committing for 30 days is at least a good starting point. During this time, you need to carve out time every day to ensure you are engaging in your new habit. You need to be consistent with your actions.

Anchor Your New Habit To An Established One

A habit should not be based on a new fad or temporary desire. It should be something that will change your life for the positive. To make habit formation simpler, you can anchor it to a routine you are already engaging in. For example, if you come home every day and change out of your work clothes, you can use this opportunity to change into some workout clothes and go for a walk or run. Another example is going to the gym after dropping the kids off at school. Try to make the new habit part of your routine.

Take Baby Steps

The only way to really make a habit stick is to turn in into automatic behavior. To do this, you can take baby steps and create low levels of commitment. The idea here is to make micro-commitments where it is almost impossible to fail. Continually increase your steps and always be consistent.

Examples of micro-commitments include:

- Walking for 5 minutes a day.
- Eating one serving of vegetables each day.
- Waking up 10 minutes earlier each morning.

Make these micro-commitments bigger each day.

Make A Plan For Obstacles

There will be plenty of obstacles along the way for any new habit formation. You must make a plan for these obstacles so they don't become major setbacks. When you know what can stop you in advance, you can take preventative action to overcome it.

Examples of obstacles include:

- Time
- Weather
- Pain
- Costs
- Space
- Illness

For example, if you know it will rain on Tuesday Afternoon when you generally go for a run, you can run in the morning instead or double up on the next day.

Create Accountability For Your Habit

Track the progress you make with your habits and make your declarations public. This way, you will be held to your commitments. If you know people are aware of your goals, then you are more likely to commit to them in order to save face. You can also get an accountability partner who will regularly follow up with you. You can also post updates on social media or in an online community group. Do whatever you can to get reinforcement from others in support of your new habit. Simply knowing you are being held accountable will keep you focused.

Reward Milestones

You don't want to wait until the end to reward yourself. The milestones you achieve along the way to your larger goal are accomplishments too. Therefore, when you reach them, reward yourself in some way. The reward does not have to break the bank. It can be small, like watching a movie, going to a restaurant, or enjoying a night out with friends. These rewards will motivate you to keep moving.

There is no way around it. The mindset you keep will determine whether or not you feel good on a regular basis. If you find yourself not feeling good, a change in mindset might be in order. This will ultimately shift your mood, which will alter your thought and change your actions. All of this will ultimately lead to a better and more productive life.

How To Stop Being A Victim

So many individuals feel bad because they turn themselves into a victim. A victim is someone who believes the world is out to get them, and they have no control over their circumstances. As a result, they start blaming other people for their setbacks and take no responsibility. I've got some news for you. If you perpetually act like a victim, you will never gain true success because you will never give yourself a chance. When you fail, you will simply believe the universe is against you. You will never understand that you have the power to change your circumstances, despite what is happening in your environment. As a victim, you will never feel good, and that is a huge problem.

The following are some ways to know if you possess the victim mindset:

- You are always making excuses for everything that is going wrong in your life.
- You always blame other people for your problems. Nothing is ever your fault.
- You always feel like you are powerless in any situation.
- You perpetually engage in negative self-talk and self-sabotage.
- You are full of anger, frustration, and resentment.
- You lack self-confidence.

Do any of these signs point to someone who will be in a positive state of well-being? Absolutely not, and that is why the victim mindset must change if you want to start feeling good. There can be many reasons for acting like a victim, like past trauma, many failed ventures, unsupportive friends, past betrayals, or being manipulated. Whatever the reason, the mindset must be done away with. The following are some ways to escape the victim mentality you may have fallen into.

Identify And Take Actionable steps To Make Improvements

If you want to start taking ownership of your life, you have to start taking active steps to make it happen. This is the only way you can improve your circumstances. For example, if you have been wallowing about not finding true love, instead of sitting around and complaining, take some action to make it happen. You will never find love until you actually look for it. Get on some dating apps, ask your friends about finding a compatible partner, or use the old school method of going out to a club and striking up a conversation. If you want to find a new job, take some positive steps to make it happen. Networking with people, building up your resume, and applying for jobs online are some of the ways you can make that new job a reality. Determine what you want to change and figure out ways to make this change occur.

Take Responsibility For Your Actions

If you make a mistake, own up to it. If you made poor decisions that put you in a bad situation, admit it, and find a way to get out of it. Will things happen that are beyond your control? Yes, but they don't have to define your results. Acknowledging your culpability is a sign of strength. It does not make you weak, but hiding things definitely does.

When you blame other people for your challenges and setbacks, it gets you nowhere fast. You may even lose important allies who had your back the whole time. When looking at a situation, recognize that things you cannot control and focus on what you can, and that is always how you respond to any circumstance. Bad things will happen to you. People will screw you over. Opportunities that were rightfully yours will be given to undeserving people. However, you can still adapt in your own way to challenges and create a great life for yourself.

Change Your Narrative

The stories we tell ourselves are the ones we end up living by. So, if we always teel ourselves stories of being stabbed in the back or finding ways to blame others, we will create that as our narrative. We must change our narrative to change our personal story. Every time you find yourself deflecting the responsibility away from you, take a moment to pause and flip the script. Instead of focusing on the issues that were out of your control, focus on the things you have the ability to change. Start asking yourself what you can do in a situation, rather than wondering why you are in that situation.

Help Others Who Are In Need

Many people with a victim mindset dwell heavily on personal hardships. They believe their problems are worse than anyone else's, and this results in them feeling helpless. If you always feel like the world is out to get you, then leave your small bubble and go out into the community. Volunteer to help people who are in need, and you will start having a different perspective on the world. This may sound counterproductive, but the more you feel deprived, the more you need to get out and help. Offer assistance to others is a great way to get out of the "Poor me" mentality.

I am not suggesting your problems are not real. However, getting out there and seeing what other people are dealing with can give you a different perspective. You will soon understand that many people are experiencing setbacks, and they can really use your help. This will make you feel more valuable, as well.

Learn To Say No

Are you someone who is always agreeing to do everything? Can someone just call you out of the blue and expect you to drop everything you are doing? Do you easily give in to the demands of other people? If so, then you need to start putting up some boundaries. The key to getting over the victim mindset is to realize that you have control over your life. You have the control to say no. You have the right to say no because your needs are important too.

Don't be afraid to refuse things. People need to know that you are not always available. If you are asked to go out with friends and don't want to, then respectfully decline the offer. There is nothing wrong with setting boundaries with people.

Change Your Circle And Change Your Mindset

You may have never thought much about who you keep in your inner circle. Many of them might be friends from your childhood, people you met at work, neighbors, friends of friends, or family members. These individuals are a major part of your life, and you may not have ever given much thought as to how they got there. More importantly, you have not given much thought to what value they bring to your life.

While I am not telling you to take advantage of your relationships, the people you surround yourself with play a significant role in your mindset, and therefore, your success. If your inner circle consists of people who carry a victim mindset, you will develop a victim mindset too. Also, spending time with like-minded people who always agree with you will never allow you to grow. The key is to find people who make you feel good about yourself and inspire you to succeed while also holding you accountable. Overall, the people you spend time with should:

- Make you a better person.
- Support you in your dreams and goals. There is a difference between harmful and helpful criticism.
- Push you to meet your goals.
- Inspire you with their own accomplishments and methodologies
- Help you transform into a new person.

While other people are not responsible for your success, they will play a role in it. This is why it's important to pay attention to the people you keep near you. While all of your connections do not have to be business-minded, they should possess certain traits that also brings the best out of you. The following are the types of people who you should keep in your inner circle if you want to start changing your mindset for the better.

The Dreamer

Dreamers are those who come up with ideas that many people do not even think of. They will literally use unimaginable ideas from their dreams and make them realistic goals. While dreamers can be seen as unrealistic, illogical, or undisciplined, they can also be true visionaries. Plus, all of the advancements we have made in the world were looked at as unrealistic by certain segments of the population. Many people could not have imagined what we've created until the final product was unveiled.

Dreamers are highly creative and can make you feel like anything is possible. If you discuss your desires with a dreamer, you can be sure they support you. In fact, they might even encourage you to dream bigger. Of course, having a dream means nothing until you take action, which brings us to the next section.

The Driver

The driver is the one who brings dreams to reality. They can see the larger picture, just like any dreamer, but also have the capability to break it down into actionable steps. Drivers are results-oriented people who are very decisive, direct, and pragmatic. They have a realistic and practical approach to life, and they know how to get things done. They thrive off the thrill of a challenge. If they want something, they will go after it. Having a driver friend or associate in your life will show you how to get things done through action. So often, we do not achieve what we want in life because we do not do the one thing we need to do, and that is to act. The driver does not let problems get in their way. They learn how to solve or get around them, and this keeps them moving forward.

The Motivator

The motivator acts as the voice of inspiration. They will keep pushing you towards your goals and will not question why you have them. They will realize that your goals are important to you and will keep motivating you to go after them. With a motivator in your life, you will become infused with energy and enthusiasm. Soon enough, it won't only be the motivator who believes in you, but you will also believe in yourself.

The Supporter

The supporter is a true friend who serves as the foundation for all of your dreams. They are the type of person whom you can let your guard around because they will not take advantage of you. You can tell them anything you want, including your deepest thoughts, and they will be your safe haven all the way through. They will comfort you during the bad times and rally for you during the better times

Having a support system like this is essential because it can seem like the whole world is against you at times. The supporter will be with you throughout your journey and give you massive encouragement the whole way through. At the very least, they will be a listening ear and a calming voice. So many people are jealous of you when you realize your success. They may not show it, but it will be there. The supporter will genuinely be happy for you and be at by your side through good and bad times. You will truly know what it means to have a real friend.

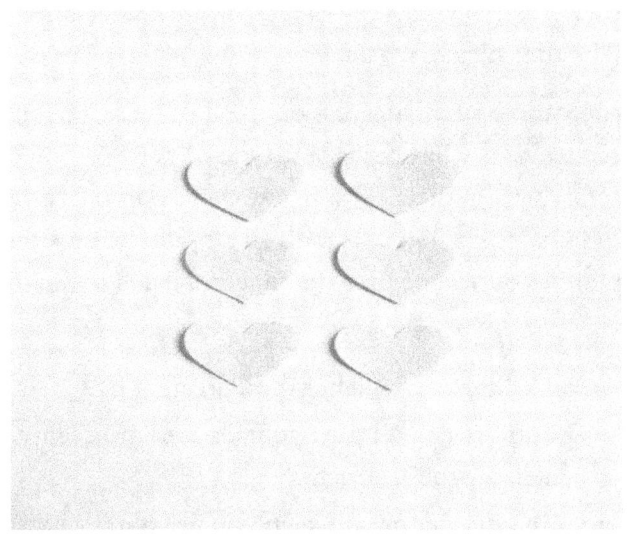

Supporters Always Show Love

The Devil's Advocate

The devil's advocate is a high-level critical thinker who can see problems well before they occur. This person asks a lot of questions because they want all of the answers that no one else is thinking about. The devil's advocate might seem like a buzzkill at first, but they are important figures to have in your life to help you view things from a different perspective.

A devil's advocate will never sugarcoat anything. They will tell you what you need to hear and not what you want to hear. In doing so, they are looking out for your best interest, so you do not get taken advantage of. They will be the voice of reason.

If you can be an amalgamation of all of these personalities, then you will be the best type of person someone else can have in their lives. If you want to improve your own inner circle, look for individuals who possess these qualities. You will be thankful that you did. To sum it all up:

- The dreamer will help you dream it up.
- The driver will turn your dream into reality by helping you take action.
- The motivator will keep you inspired every step of the way.
- The support will stay by your side through good and bad times. They will be your most loyal friend. Treat them well.
- The devil's advocate will be the real deal who tells you like it is. They will cut through the nonsense.

Of course, creating your inner circle involves knowing who you don't want in there. The following are some of the types who want to avoid and even extricate from your surroundings, no matter who they are or how long you have known them. No relationship is worth destroying your opportunity to feel good.

Manipulators

These very toxic individuals are great at twisting people's minds around for their own benefits. These individuals will pretend to be your friend, but it is a façade to deceive you in some way. Sometimes, it is quite obvious, while other times, you may never know. Manipulators know what you like, what makes you happy and can make you laugh. They know how to be charming so they can get you on their side. All of this is done to extract more information about you, which they plan on using against you at some point.

Be very careful because they will do anything to win you over. For example, they will do nice things for you to place guilt trips on you for bigger favors they will need in the future. It is best to avoid manipulative people because you will expend too much energy fighting with them later. The following are a few ways to spot a manipulator:

- They try to do too much for you too soon.
- They are always playing the victim. Nothing in their lives is ever their fault.
- Their actions do not match their words. They will tell you what you want to hear but will flake out when it comes to action.

- They will always make you feel guilty. They are masters at leveraging your guilt to their advantage.
- They will quickly agree to help, but then act like a martyr when they do. For example, they will offer to help you with a task, like moving, and then remind you how tired they are every step of the way like they are moving the earth for you.
- They will always try to one-up you with their problems.

Criticizers

There is such a thing as constructive criticism or feedback. This is done with the intent to be helpful. Some criticism can bring you down and completely ruin your mood and drive. Toxic criticizers will always find a way to tell you your effort or results were not good enough. They are constantly negative and pessimistic, and if you are around them long enough, you will eventually feel like you are never good enough. These types of toxic people will become a hindrance as you are trying to grow. Learn to ignore them because no matter what you do, they will find a way to tell you it was not good enough.

Gossipers

"Great minds discuss ideas, average ones discuss events, and small minds discuss people."

-Eleanor Roosevelt

Honestly, everyone gossips to a certain degree. It's natural to do so and often a slip of the tongue. If you find yourself gossiping regularly, you need to pull back. If you are around a gossiper, you must distance yourself from them. Being around a gossiper is a waste of time that brings no value and can also corrupt your mind.

Also, always remember that someone who will gossip to you will gossip about you. How do you know that a person who's telling you everyone's dirty laundry is not turning around and airing your dirty laundry too? There is no way to know, and you just have to assume that's what they are doing. Gossiping becomes part of their personality and makeup, which makes these individuals truly toxic.

You can easily spot a gossiper if they are nice to people to their face but talk bad about them behind their back.

Self-Absorbed

Self-absorbed people only care about themselves. They believe the world owes them something and nothing else matters unless they get what they want. Whatever they think, do, or say is always surrounding them. It is okay to care for yourself. In fact, it is a necessity for wellbeing. Self-absorbed people take it to another level, though. They literally only care about themselves and have no interest in the rest of the world.

Be careful around self-absorbed people because they will always have their own interest at heart, even if it's to your detriment. To spot a self-absorbed person, recognize the following characteristics:

- They are always on the defensive. They never want to see the world from another person's perspective and simply want to see it through theirs to protect their flaws and image.
- They don't see the big picture and think the world is just about them.
- They always want to dominate any relationships they are in because they see them as tools for getting what they want.
- They often feel insecure.
- They always believe and act like they are superior to others.
- They are highly opinionated and ignore what other people think.
- Their relationships do not usually last long because they are heavily one-sided.
- They don't have a real sense of empathy.

Envious

Envious people are jealous of others' success, happiness, achievements, and attention. Instead of being happy for what they have and who they are, they constantly measure their fortune against everyone else in the world. Envious people will always make sure no one is better than them. It is not something they can handle.

Being around these types of toxic personalities can be harmful because they will teach you to underestimate your endeavors. They can talk you out of living your dreams because they don't want you to achieve success. They look at your success as their failure.

Needy

Needy people are those who are always asking for one thing or another. If you give them something, they will just ask for more. For example, they may ask you to loan them some money to buy groceries. Before you know it, they will be asking for help in paying large bills and will start needing money every single week. There is nothing wrong with helping someone who truly needs it. However, there is a difference between needing something during an emergency and just being needy. It's a good idea to stay away from habitually needy people because they will ultimately drain you of your resources. Furthermore, they will make you feel guilty when you can't help them.

Temperamental

Temperamental people are those who have no control over their emotions. They can lash out at any time for any reason and completely lose control. It's easy to feel bad for these individuals because of how they behave, but you must be careful not to get caught up in their trap. These individuals are very toxic and can ruin your ability to stay focused. All of us have the capability to lose it at some point, especially during times of great stress. For temperamental people, it is a part of who they are.

Dementors

Dementors are the type of toxic people who can walk into a room and suck all of the energy out of it. There is something about their demeanor, attitude, or overall energy that turns them into energy-sucking vampires. If you notice your mood and energy get depleted almost instantly around certain people, those people have qualities of being a dementor and should be avoided at all costs. While it can be hard to control who comes into a room during a crowd, you don't have to get close to these people.

Liars

It's pretty easy to see why these individuals are not fun to be around. People who are habitual liars can never be trusted. It is hard to know when and if they are ever forthcoming with you and what types of things they are hiding. Liars can even make up things about you and other people, which creates unnecessary tension within several different groups. It is one thing to lie or withhold information to spare someone's feelings. For example, if someone cooks for you and it doesn't taste great, you might still tell them it is good because they put in the effort to make you something. Chronic and habitual liars take it to a whole other level, to the point it becomes pathological.

Slackers

Slackers are extremely frustrating to be around. They lounge around all day, never getting any work down, and just want to be lazy. Instead of doing things themselves, they try to get other people to do them. Being around someone who always avoids work can be very discouraging and demotivating. What makes it worse, slackers will get you to do their work for them and somehow take the credit for it. Slackers will not bring any value to your life and will ultimately increase your workload. Avoid these toxic people. Don't try to understand them. Just work hard on your own things and let them deal with whatever they need to do.

> "I can't relate to lazy people. We don't speak the same language. I don't understand you. I don't want to understand you."
> -Kobe Bryant

Always remember that the people you keep in your life will affect your mindset. Your mindset affects your thoughts, your thoughts affect your actions, and your actions create your results. Finally, your results determine whether you feel good or not. By targeting the mindset, you are targeting the core of what you need to feel good.

Chapter 5: The Power Of Self-Care

Self-care is described as any activity aimed at improving our own health and wellbeing. This concept is extremely important but sorely missing in so many people's lives because they are busy and stressed with all of their responsibilities. The only time many people take care of themselves is when they are sick, and sometimes, this is not even the case. Between the hectic schedules, stressful jobs, family responsibilities, and being too consumed with technology, it becomes impossible for individuals to take care of the most important person in their lives: Themselves. This is something that needs to change immediately if we are to start feeling good.

Benefits Of Self-Care

There are many benefits of self-care, the most obvious being that it makes people feel better. The following are a few other important benefits of self-care, which illustrate why it should not be ignored if we want to improve.

Slowing Down Makes You More Productive

Slowing down can mean several things. It can mean not always picking up that extra shift at work. It can be saying "no" to going for a night out on the town. It could also mean taking an afternoon nap. All of these moments used to slow down help bring us back to the present moment. These moments give us time to become centered and reprioritize our tasks. You will also be able to reenergize, which will make you more productive in the long run. If you never take time to slow down, you will eventually burn out your engine.

Self-Care Will Boost Your Immune System

Are you someone who is always getting sick, whether it is the sniffles, aches, and pain, headaches, or other common symptoms? Your problem might be that you never take care of yourself, so your immune system is not functioning optimally. Relaxation activities, whatever they may be, activate your parasympathetic nervous system, which puts your body into a state of rest. This gives our bodies a chance to restore and decompress from our hectic lives. Therefore, your immune system will have an opportunity to build its defense system against the microbes that try to infect us during our weakest moments. Once you increase the self-care activities in your life, the number of sick days will eventually go down.

Self-Care Improve Self-Compassion

This is a pretty simple formula: The more you take care of yourself, the better you will feel. Self-compassion means we are kinder to ourselves when we suffer, fail, or feel inadequate. We avoid self-criticizing. The key here is to listen to the way you speak in your mind and realize that you would never talk to someone else that way. Therefore, you need to start showing the same compassion for yourself that you show to other people.

You'll Find Out More About Who You Are

How many times do you stop and wonder what you love to do and what things in life make you happy? Unfortunately, many people cannot answer this question well because they rarely take the time to think about it. We are conditioned to think about other people all the time and believe any thoughts of self are considered selfish. Well, this is not the case, and you must stop thinking in this manner. When you engage in self-care, you learn more about who you are because you take the time to learn what you love. As you open up to self-care, you will begin to love yourself more.

You Will Have More To Give To Others

Imagine this for a moment: You have a glass, and you begin pouring the contents into other glasses until the original one is empty. Now the glass is sitting there and can no longer give to any other glass. It will be a while until the glass can be refilled. This same analogy holds true for people. If we constantly give to others and never take time to refuel, we will eventually run dry and have nothing left to give. However, if we give a little and take time to refuel, then we can give continuously without really slowing down. Basically, when you take care of yourself, then you will have more to give to other people. If you don't, you will eventually burn out and will no longer be able to help anybody.

On top of these benefits, self-care can help avoid many chronic illnesses, unmanageable stress, anxiety and help us always feel on top of our game. Never ignore the extreme benefits of self-care. Doing so will lead to detrimental consequences in the end.

How To Engage In Self-Care

For those of you who have never committed to self-care probably don't have a clue of how it's done. Fortunately, there are many activities to go over that will help get the ball rolling for you. Basically, if something puts you into a state of relaxation and helps you feel better, it's probably a fairly good self-care practice.

Sleep

Make sleep a part of your self-care routine. Never dismiss the benefits of getting uninterrupted sleep, whether at night or an afternoon nap. Sleep can affect the way you feel, both physically and emotionally. Without it, you will feel sluggish and often irritable. Stress and various distractions can put a damper on your sleep cycle. Furthermore, habits like a poor diet or scrolling through social media can ruin a restful night.

To develop good sleeping habits, think about your nightly routine. What activities are you engaging in right before bed, and are those having an impact on you? If so, work to eliminate these activities. Make sure your bedroom is conducive to a restful night's sleep. Therefore, put any items that create a distraction, like the TV or mobile device, outside. Keep the environment as peaceful as possible.

Take Care Of Your Gut

Digestive health is often ignored when we think about our wellbeing. However, your gut health plays a significant role in your health and vitality. Think about how sluggish you feel when you are bloated or experiences any digestive issues. They are not comfortable and can impede many of your activities of daily living. The types of food you eat will affect the bacteria in your digestive tract, and this will create a cascade of either positive or negative outcomes. Pay attention to what you eat and how it makes you feel. Healing the gut can make you a happy person.

Exercise Daily

Exercise is definitely good for us, but do you realize how good it actually is? Daily exercise will boost your mood, give you energy, reduce stress and anxiety, improve your self-esteem, and help you with image consciousness when you lose weight. Once again, choose the activities that you enjoy and fit your schedule the best.

Take A Self-Care Trip

With a self-care trip, you are getting away from your familiar surroundings for a while and using this time to disconnect. This will help you relax and get rejuvenated. These trips do not have to be costly. It can just mean driving to the next town over and hanging out for a couple of hours or going on a weekend getaway. The goal with these trips is to veer away from your regular schedule and take the time to do something for yourself.

Step Outside For a Bit

Stepping outside for a while can help reduce stress, lower blood pressure, and make you more mindful. Going out into some fresh air can even give you extra energy. If you are feeling that afternoon slump, instead of drinking an extra coffee, try going for a five-minute walk and see how you feel after that. You can also go for a hike, walk in the park, or do some gardening.

Get A Pet

A pet can help boost our lives by bringing in happiness. Most people go for dogs or cats but get whatever animal you think you can take care of. Animals will give unconditional love and provide great companionship. They are also great for reducing anxiety and help people with disorders like PTSD or depression. Service animals are now being used for emotional support, which has been helpful for a lot of people.

Get Organized

Getting organized can help create a healthier you. It allows you to figure out what you already have and what you still need. Small changes, like getting a planner, clearing out your desk, cleaning the kitchen, or doing that pile of laundry, are all great ways to get organized. Also, make sure your essential items, like keys, wallets, backpacks, and coats, are always in the same place every day.

Cook At Home

With our busy schedules, it is much more convenient to stop by a drive-thru restaurant and pick up some quick food rather than cooking a healthy meal at home. These fast meals are not usually sufficient in the nutrients your body needs and are often loaded with chemicals. Sopping by the drive-thru all the time will not be good for your health or overall wellbeing. Consider making more healthy meals, even if it's just a few times a week. You can also order meal kits from various delivery services, which are healthier than fast food.

Block Out Time For Self-Care

While you are loading up that planner with all of your essential activities, make sure to block out specific times for self-care. For example, write down that you will stop working at 7 PM every night and read a fun book or spend time with family. Once you block off this time, guard it with everything you have. That means you refuse offers to go out from friends or anything else that can disrupt this self-care time. Unless it's an emergency, do not give in.

These are just examples of ways to incorporate self-care into your life. You can use these as examples to come up with others.

Mindfulness

I have mentioned mindfulness a few times throughout this book, and I want to explore it more deeply here since it is an essential practice for self-care. Mindfulness is the basic ability to be fully present in our current situations. When we are mindful, we are aware of what is happening, what we're doing, and where we are. As a result, we are able to objectively look at our surroundings and not become overly reactive to what is going on around us.

Everyone has the ability to be mindful, but it's more readily available when we practice it on a daily basis. Whenever you bring awareness to what you're directly experiencing with your senses, your thoughts, or your emotions, you are actively mindful. The goal of mindfulness is to wake up to the inner workings of your physical, mental, emotional, and spiritual processes. Basically, you are living where you are meant to be, which in the present moment and not the past or future.

Benefits Of Mindfulness

Mindfulness can bring many different benefits to your life. As you go through these, you will see how the practice can help you deal with many daily struggles we all go through. Mindfulness will give you the advantage of being ahead of the game by being able to handle whatever comes your way with clarity and efficiency. That being said, here are some of the major benefits of being mindful:

- Decreased stress: Stress is a topic that has come up a lot already, and there is a good reason for that. While some stress is necessary, an overabundance of it will negatively affect our wellbeing in every aspect. Controlling stress allows you to feel better on a regular basis.
- Being able to handle illnesses. We cannot fully control our health. We can take many precautionary measures to reduce risk factors, but that

does not mean disease will not find us in some way. Mindfulness will put you in a mental state where you are more capable of handling and managing illnesses, whether they are chronic or short-term.

- It can facilitate a quicker recovery. Not only will mindfulness allow us to deal with illness while we are going through it, but it also equips us with the ability to move forward once the illness is gone. This is because we objectively realize what we need to do and stop getting in our own way.
- Mindfulness has long been considered a supplemental treatment for depression. One of the main reasons is because the practitioner is able to better regulate their emotions.
- Mindfulness can improve your focus and concentration. This will allow you to improve your performance and productivity.
- You will be able to appreciate the beauty of the world because you will actually slow down to take it all in.
- When you practice mindfulness activities at night, it results in better sleep.
- When you practice mindfulness first thing in the morning, it gives you extra energy to start your day.

- When you practice mindfulness in the afternoon, it gives you that extra surge to finish out your day.
- It gives you the ability to see your goals more clearly.

There are numerous other benefits that come from mindfulness, and research is continuing to find more. This list is just the beginning of what you can accomplish through this exercise.

Mindfulness Practices

Now that you understand the benefits of mindfulness, I will go over some specific techniques you can use on a daily basis. Many of these exercises can be practiced just about anywhere because they are simple.

- Perform a mindful body scan. This type of scan is a great way to get in touch with how you are feeling. To perform this, start at the feet and slowly move up while focusing on each area of the body. As you are focusing, determine how the area feels. Note any pain, tingling, numbness, or other unusual sensations.

- Practice a morning breathing exercise. Practicing mindful breathing for just a few minutes a day can help reduce stress and promote relaxation. Take slow, rhythmic breaths that help activate the parasympathetic nervous system. This will cause all of your body processes, including your heart rate and breathing, to slow down.

- Practice shower meditation. If a shower is already part of your routine, use this time to practice some mindfulness. You can focus on deep thinking and create positive thoughts for the rest of the day.

- Writing your thoughts in a journal is a great way to focus on what is going on in your mind. You can liberate yourself from all of the mental chatter that is happening and recognize what thoughts are really important to you.

- Create a tea or coffee ritual. Many people just stumble to the coffee machine, pour a cup, and gulp it down quickly while trying not to burn their tongue. Use this time to actually slow down and enjoy our cup of coffee or tea.

- Just like with your coffee and tea ritual, take time to enjoy your breakfast too. Sit down and take in your meal. This will allow you to assess your food choices, as well.

- Be present with your family. When you are sitting down with your family, whether it's at the dinner table, driving in a car, or watching a movie, be fully present with them instead of playing on the phone or taking care of business.

- Connect with nature whenever you go outside. This does not just mean going for a hike. So often, we are running from one place to another, and we forget that there is a world around us. Whenever you are walking outside from one place to another, take a few seconds to soak everything in. Smell the flowers, feel the warmth of the sun, and take in the various sounds that you hear.

- When you are driving, practice mindfulness. When you get in the car, take a few deep breaths before you start driving. As you are driving, make an effort to notice your surroundings. Keep the radio turned off and avoid the Bluetooth. Notice the various feelings that arise if you are stuck in traffic. Take more deep breath before getting out of your car.

- Practice transition breathing. This means that when you are moving on from one task or project to the next, take a few deep and purposeful breaths to help calm your nerves a little bit. This is especially helpful before jumping into a highly stressful situation.

- Focus on your work purpose. Why do you work? Is it just to pay the bills, or do you have some higher purpose? Being mindful of the purpose of your work allows you to be more engaged with every task you perform.

- The Pomodoro Technique is a great way to increase productivity. The idea is to break work down into 25-minute intervals, which are called Pomodoros. After the 25-minutes, you take a five-minute break. After 4 Pomodoros, you take a 15 or 30-minute break.

- Decrease distractions by putting away your phone and other devices when you don't need it, clear your desk, and avoid answering emails when you don't have to.

- Be present with your peers. This can help improve your work environment and communication.

- Stand, stretch, and get moving often. Avoid sitting in one place for too long. Get away from this environment for a while and go move around.

- Take a break from your digital devices. With the way we are attached to our phones, this seems impossible to many. However, you do not need to have your devices on you at all times. When you need a break, take a break.

- Practice a shut-down ritual. Practice some mindfulness habits within the last hour before you go to bed, like meditation, prayer, or deep breathing.

- Start an evening gratitude journal where you think about and write down all of the things you are grateful for on that day.

These are just a few mindfulness exercises for you to practice. The goal with all of these is to slow down and become present in whatever moment you are in. You will be amazed at how much mental clarity you receive and the increase in energy you have.

Decluttering

Decluttering is a practice where you remove unnecessary items from your life. Over the years, we tend to build up our material possessions, and they end up just sitting in one place, never to be used again. This could be because we no longer need them or never needed them in the first place. Decluttering is more than just clearing out for extra space. There are actually several mental health benefits to it, as well. When you live in a more organized environment, you feel a sense of mental clarity. In addition, you will have the following benefits:

- Less debt
- More space
- More freedom
- Less stress
- More money

Decluttering is a simple process but difficult for people to do because they have a strange connection to their personal belongings. Here are some helpful tips to start decluttering your life right away.

- Start with just five minutes a day. If you are new to decluttering, spend five minutes on your first day decluttering and removing certain items from your home. You can build up from here.
- Give one item away each day. By the end of the first year, you will have given away 365 items. If you want to speed up the process, you can always give away two or more items.
- Get a trash bag, go around your house, and fill it up as fast as you can. Whatever items you collect can be donated to Goodwill.
- Take the 12-12-12 challenge. Go around your house and locate 12 items to throw away, 12 items to donate, and 12 items to keep.
- View your home as a first-time visitor. The reason we have so many items is that we have a hard time parting with them. When we bought an item in the past, we either needed it or wanted it at that time. However, looking at it now, it is not something we would ever purchase. Therefore, walk into your house with the mindset of a first-time visitor and decide what items you would actually want if you saw them in a store today. The rest can be sold or given away.

- Take before and after photos of a small area in your home. For example, take a picture of your desk before removing the clutter, and then quickly remove the items in the picture so you can take another photo. Compare the two and see how your house could look after decluttering.

Decluttering not only improves your mental health but your physical health too. Having fewer items in your home allows fewer chances for dust and mite buildup, which can lead to respiratory issues in the future.

The Benefits Of Exercise

Exercise is another topic we have mentioned throughout this book, as it has many benefits related to feeling good. Exercise is defined as any movement that raises your heart rate, gets your muscles moving, and causes your body to burn calories. You can get creative with what your exercise routines will be. The focus of this section will be to deeply explore the benefits of exercise and why you must include it in your schedule for overall wellbeing.

It Can Make You Feel Happier

Exercise has been shown to increase mood and reduce feelings of depression, stress, anxiety, and other mood disorders. It targets the areas of the brain, regular stress, and anxiety. In addition, the feel-good hormones like serotonin and endorphins are released, which leads to a feeling of happiness, as well.

Your mood can benefit greatly, no matter how intense your routine is. Therefore, a simple walk in the park or around the block can make you feel happier. In a study done with a sample size of 26 healthy men and women who exercised regularly, half were asked to stop exercising while the other half were asked to continue. After two weeks, the group that stopped exercising showed increased signs of depression.

The next time you are feeling bummed out, trying to do some type of physical activity, you enjoy and see how you feel afterward.

It Can Help With Weight Loss

Weight loss is an obvious reason for starting an exercise regimen. Losing excess weight will lead to improved energy, reduced risk of chronic illnesses, and a better self-image. When you look at yourself in the mirror after losing significant amounts of healthy weight, you feel rather good about yourself. A good exercise program is combining aerobic exercise with resistance training. This will maximize fat loss and maintain muscle mass.

Great For Your Muscles And Bones

Exercise releases hormones that promote the ability of your muscles to absorb amino acids. The amino acids help them grow and reduces breakdown. Exercise can also help build bone density. With the increase in muscle mass and bone density, a person is less likely to obtain musculoskeletal injuries.

High impact exercises like gymnastics or running have been shown to promote higher bone density that non-impact exercises like swimming or cycling.

It Can Help With Brain Health And Memory

Exercise increases blood flow to the rest of the body, including the brain. It also stimulates the production of hormones that enhance the growth of brain cells. Finally, regular physical activity will promote changes in brain structure and function.

In relation to memory, exercise has been shown to increase the size of the hippocampus. This portion of the brain is vital for learning and memory.

It Can Help With Relaxation And Sleep Quality

The energy depletion that occurs during exercise stimulates the recuperative process during sleep. The increase in body temperature from a good workout can also lead to improved sleep quality because the temperature slowly drops during the sleep cycle, resulting in more restful sleep. The complete physiology behind this is not known; however, many studies have confirmed the benefits that exercise has on sleep quality.

In a sample study, it was found that 150 minutes of moderate-to-vigorous exercise can lead to a 65% improvement in sleep quality.

Sleep Better At Night

I will end this self-care chapter by going over one of the most necessary things for feeling good, and that is getting proper sleep. Humans need their bedtime hours; otherwise, they will become worthless as far as productivity. Poor sleep habits can also lead to many chronic illnesses. So, make sure you are doing your best to get a restful night's sleep. The following are some tips to help you get going.

Increase Your Bright Light Exposure During The Day

Your body has a natural time-keeping clock known as the circadian rhythm, which affects your body, brain, and hormones. This rhythm tells your body when to stay awake and when to go to sleep. When you get more light exposure during the day, especially natural light, it helps to keep your circadian rhythm healthy. This increases your daytime energy and improves your nighttime sleep quality.

During a study of adults with insomnia, higher exposure to bright lights during the day improved both sleep quality and duration. The time it took to fall asleep also decreased by 83%. While most of the sleep studies that exist out there are with people who have sleep disorders, it is expected that similar results would occur even if you experience average sleep.

Reduce Blue Light Exposure During The Evening

Excessive blue light exposure during the evening will completely throw off your circadian rhythm because it tricks your brain into thinking it's still daytime. This reduces hormones that help you fall asleep, like melatonin.

Blue light comes from electronic devices like computers and smartphones. If you must use these devices in the evening, there are a few tricks to reduce the amount of exposure you have:

- Wear glasses that block blue light.
- Install an app that blocks blue lights on your smartphone.
- If possible, turn off any electronics about two hours before you go to bed.

Avoid Extra Caffeine Consumption

Caffeine has numerous health benefits when taken in small doses. Caffeine also gives you energy, so consuming it late in the day can severely impact your sleep cycle. It is recommended that you avoid any caffeine six hours before going to bed.

Reduce Taking Long Naps

A good nap during the day can be quite refreshing. If it's a quick power nap that lasts 20-30 minutes, then it's no big deal. However, extended naps that last several hours can confuse your timeclock, which makes it difficult to fall asleep at night. If you are feeling tired during the day, try going for a walk. If you must nap, don't let it last for more than 30 minutes. Quickly recharge your battery and get moving again.

Be Consistent With Your Sleep/Wake Cycles

The circadian rhythm functions on a set loop and aligns itself with the sunrise and sunset. When you sleep and wake up at the same time every day, your body maintains a consistent rhythm that it's used to, and this leads to better sleep quality. Even on your days off, it is recommended you avoid changing your sleep/wake cycle.

Take A Melatonin Supplement

While I don't recommend taking sleep aids like Benadryl of alcoholic beverages, melatonin is a supplement that is also found naturally as a hormone in your body. This sleep hormone tells your brain when it's time to relax and head to bed. Melatonin is also known to not have any withdrawal effects.

If you go this route, start with a low dose to see your tolerance, and increase slowly as needed. Even though melatonin is found naturally in the body, it also alters brain chemistry, so it is recommended you see a medical professional before starting up a regimen.

Don't Drink Alcohol At Night

Many people will drink at night to help them relax after a long day. However, alcohol can disrupt your sleep cycles and hormones. For example, it can alter your nighttime melatonin production, which will also disrupt your circadian rhythm. Alcohol has also been shown to cause sleep apnea and snoring. Avoid drinking alcohol at night before going to bed.

Optimize Your Bedroom Environment

Your bedroom setup is a key factor in getting a good night's sleep. Therefore, make sure the temperature is comfortable, the noise is down to a minimum, there are no external lights (get light-blocking curtains if needed), and the furniture arrangement should be optimal. Manage these aspects well, and you will find yourself getting restful sleep.

Don't Eat Late In The Evening

Eating late at night can affect the natural release of melatonin and disrupt your sleep quality. If you get hungry, a small, healthy snack like carrot sticks, Greek yogurt, or a handful of nuts is recommended over a chocolate bar, chips, or a heavy meal.

Relax And Clear Your Mind

You worked hard all day, so use the last couple of hours before going to bed to relax and wind down. Don't think about work and any struggles you may be having. Save those for the next day. This is the perfect time to practice some of the mindfulness techniques I discussed earlier.

Take A Relaxing Bath Or Shower

Taking a warm shower or bath in the evening can help relax your muscles and calm your nerves. It will be a huge mood booster, as well, so you will have a peaceful night's sleep.

Check Out Your Bed, Pillow, And Blanket

Have you ever been to a hotel and notice that you sleep better? This is probably because they have higher-quality beds, pillows, and blankets than you do at home. For the sake of getting some good sleep, make sure to invest in these items. It may cost you a little more upfront, but it will be worth it for many years of proper sleep.

Avoid Liquids Before Bed

You know that when you sleep, your internal organs don't. They are continuously working to make sure you stay alive. This is a great thing, but you also make urine during the night. Having to get up to use the restroom can interrupt a peaceful sleep pattern. For this reason, avoid drinking heavy amounts of liquid within two hours of going to bed.

Volunteering And Why It Makes You Feel Good

When you volunteer, you are selflessly helping someone or a group who needs you at that moment. It is a great feeling to know you were able to help someone during their time of need. Volunteering benefits the recipient heavily. However, they are not the only ones it benefits. When you volunteer, you also receive many benefits that come from helping others, and all of these contribute to you feeling good. Being a volunteer can actually be a great self-care activity.

Volunteering Connects You With Others

Volunteering can have a tremendous impact on the community. As well, it allows you to connect with members of the said community and build positive relationships. You can unite with people over a common cause that you believe in and expand your network of friends and associates. Volunteering can also increase your social and relationship skills.

Volunteering Is Beneficial For Your Body And Mind

There are many positive benefits to your mental and physical health that come from volunteering. Helping others and the community can counteract the effects of stress, anxiety, and other negative emotions. Meaningful connections with other human beings are great for relieving stress.

Researchers have actually found that being helpful to others brings immense pleasure, and this can be seen by measuring certain hormones and brain activity. Volunteering can also:

- Increase your self-confidence, which comes with being able to help people.
- Provide a sense of purpose as helping others gives life new meaning.
- Help you stay active and ready for challenges.

Volunteering Can Advance your Career

Volunteering is a great way to pick up new skills, whether they are specific to a certain industry or more generalized, like social skills, teamwork, problem-solving, and good customer service. After some time, you can start using the skills you obtain while volunteering at your place of work. This can eventually lead to promotions or a new career path.

Volunteering Brings Fun And Fulfillment To Your Life

Volunteering is a great way to explore your interests and passions in life. It also provides you with renewed creativity, motivation, and vision that can transition over to your personal and professional life. Finally, volunteering can allow you to engage in fun hobbies while also giving back to the community. For example, if you love animals, you can volunteer at an animal shelter. If you love nature, you can help plant a community garden.

Volunteering provides many immense benefits for you, and there are many opportunities available for you to get involved. To find the right opportunity for you, ask yourself the following questions:

- What specific causes do I care about?
- Do I want to improve anything in my own neighborhood?
- Do I want to meet new people who are different from me?
- What do I enjoy doing in my spare time?
- What types of things do I enjoy enough to do for free?
- What skills do I have that I can share with other people?

The best way to volunteer is to find something that matches your personality and interests. These questions will help narrow that down.

Stress Management Techniques

Stress is a common part of life and, in many instances, is needed to overcome obstacles in life. For example, the stress response is essential during any fight-or-flight response as a safety mechanism to get out of danger. Stress can give us strength and energy to overcome many challenges. Minimal amounts of stress are needed to keep us alert and prevent us from becoming lazy. Stress is a good thing in small doses. However, long-term stress can be detrimental to our mental and physical health. If you are constantly stressed out, there is no way that you can feel good about anything in life. The following are a few stress management techniques to keep your stress under control, so you can feel good on a more regular basis.

Maintain A Positive Attitude

It is very easy to focus on all of the negative things in life. Our minds tend to revert to these negative thoughts automatically. As a result, we go into a state of chronic stress and worry about everything. No matter what blessings we have, we always think about the bad things going on. To maintain a positive attitude, you must challenge these thoughts in real-time and replace them with positive ones. Anytime you feel a negative thought coming on, actively stop it in its tracks and think about a blessing that you have in life. Maintaining a positive attitude will go a long way in managing stress.

Accept What You Cannot Control

People often take the weight of the world on their shoulders. Even the events that are in no way their faults become a burden. In order to reduce stress, you have to accept that many things are beyond your control, and worrying about will do you no good. You can't change them anyway. These types of things include:

- World events
- The Weather
- Other people's actions
- People's onions
- What the future holds

While you cannot control these things, you can control how you react to them, which is where your energy needs to go. If you spend too much time trying to change things you can't control, you will just get burned out.

Be Assertive, Not Aggressive

There is a lot of misconceptions about being assertive. It simply means you are clear, confident, and straightforward in how you communicate. It does not mean you are aggressive or rude in any way. Assert your feelings, opinions, and beliefs, so people know what's going on in your mind and also get all of your feeling off your chest.

Make Time For Hobbies

All work and no play make people sad and angry. Rightfully so because life is meant to be enjoyed. If you work all the time and never engage in any hobbies or fun activities, you will only build up your stress levels until you explode. It's like letting a pressure working go on forever until it actually bursts. Once in a while, the pressure needs to be released, and the same goes for you. Let yourself decompress to relieve stress and tension. Always make time for hobbies and relaxation.

Learn To Manage Your Time

Time management is an overlooked skill that is essential for any type of success in life. Time management leads to better productivity and performance. In addition, it leads to reduced stress. When you don't manage your time well, everything goes into disarray, and you cannot keep all of your tasks organized. Eventually, this will all lead to more stress. Once you learn proper time management techniques, your stress levels will also go down.

In addition to these strategies, self-care practices, in general, are great for managing stress. Always take the time for self-care and never let anyone tell you it's not important.

I know I covered a lot of information in this chapter, but the main takeaway is that self-care is essential, and there are many aspects of it. Never put your self-care on the back burner because it is needed to keep your battery charged and to keep feeling good. Self-care is not selfish, and you must always remember that.

Self-Care

Chapter 6: When To Get Professional Help

There will be times where simple techniques you can engage in at home will not be enough. Your mental and emotional status will get so out of control that you won't be able to bring it together. When this occurs, it may be time for you to seek professional help. There can be many forms of professional help available, from licensed therapists, counselors, social workers, spiritual advisors, or life coaches. All of these professionals have their unique talents, and they can help you in different ways. I will go over these different fields and let you know when to seek each one of them out. Before I get there, let's talk about the stigma that still exists regarding asking for help.

Feeling isolated

Stigma Of Asking For Help

Stigma occurs when something is viewed as negative by the general public. Hence, there is a stigma surrounding asking for help, mainly in regard to getting therapy. For many decades, and maybe even centuries, the idea of seeking out help through counseling has been looked down upon as being weak. Those who seek this kind of help have no control over their lives and are just asking like drama queens. Many people believe they don't have willpower. While mindsets are changing regarding these philosophies, the negative perceptions still exist.

Stigmas can lead to a lot of discrimination. The discrimination can be more direct, like someone outwardly mocking or making negative remarks towards someone, or more passive, like avoiding someone who suffers from mental illness or anguish. Unfortunately, many of those who need professional help take these negative attitudes to heart. There are many consequences related to the stigma:

- Reluctance to seek any help or treatment. Why would someone want to get help if they will be mocked for it?
- Lack of understanding from family, friends, and others in the community. Mental health is still largely unknown by the general population.
- Bullying, harassment, and violence towards people who are suffering because they are looked at as weak.
- Fewer opportunities for work, school, and social activities. Either because the person is suffering too much to be functional, or the people around him/her don't want to deal with the issues.
- Health insurance can often be limited when it comes to treatment for mental health.
- A belief that certain challenges will never be met because you do not have the capability of dealing with them.

The following are some steps to start dealing with the stigma.

Get Treatment

One of the most obvious steps in overcoming the stigma is to just bypass it and get treatment. Once you receive treatment, you will get to the root of your problems and start feeling better. The benefits you receive from therapy will help you overcome the feelings of being stigmatized as you will start feeling better about yourself. Just remember, it is better to ask for help early than harm yourself later because you were worried about looking weak.

Don't Let The Stigma Create Self-Doubt

Stigma does not just come from outside sources. We often have a stigma about seeking help in our own minds. We talk ourselves into believing that if we go to therapy, it makes us weak. Don't let your mind think in this manner. Receiving help in the form of therapy is not weak. It is actually a sign of strength. Seeking counseling, education, or assistance in any way can help improve your self-esteem and prevent self-doubt.

Avoid Isolating

Whatever your reason may be for isolating yourself, don't do it. Instead, reach out to people you trust, like family, friends, clergy, members of your community, and, if needed, a therapist. These individuals can offer you support if they know about your mental illness. If they don't know, they can't help you. Even if you have not been diagnosed with a mental illness, if you are feeling rotten and not yourself, seek out the help of others. Don't isolate because this only suppresses your negative emotions. I am pretty sure your friends would rather be annoyed by your stories than have to read negative stories about you later on.

Don't Let Your Mental Health Define You

You are not an illness, a negative emotion, or anything else similar. You are a human being who happens to be dealing with these challenges. Don't define yourself by them.

Join A Support Group

There are many national and local support groups that offer education about various mental illnesses. Attending meetings for these groups can go a long way in reducing the stigma related to mental health. These groups and resources are available to everyone, whether suffering from mental health or not.

Speak Out Against Stigma

If you are willing, speak out against the stigma in your own way. If you can get public speeches somewhere, go for it. In modern times, you can easily make a video for online consumption, whether it's on YouTube, Facebook, or anywhere else videos are available.

The goal of all of these methods is to offer information to the public so there is a better understanding of mental health issues. If you are dealing with a mental health issue or just having a hard time regulating your emotions, it's important to recognize what you are going through, don't be ashamed of it, and seek support. If you know someone facing these challenges, it's important to be supportive and assist them in getting help. If you can't help them, at least don't get in their way.

Why Vulnerability Is Strength

Many individuals who are suffering from emotional or mental issues feel like asking for help, and putting their problems out in the world is weak. They don't want to make themselves vulnerable out of fear. As a result, they feel bottling everything up and remaining stoic is the way to go. However, being vulnerable is actually a sign of strength. When you are vulnerable, you are taking a risk by putting yourself out there for the world to see. You have the chance of being exposed, harmed, or insulted.

It is similar to staying in your home because you are scared versus going outside and facing the world. When you refuse to be vulnerable, you are staying indoors and protecting yourself. Therefore, when you feel bad for acting vulnerable and think you are showing weakness, you are acting stronger than you realize. The following are a few reasons why vulnerability should be embraced rather than shunned.

Vulnerability Allows Advancement

Whenever you try something new, it can be a frightening moment. You won't know how things turn out and, therefore, you are making yourself vulnerable. Putting yourself in this position is essential for any type of advancement in life. You will not reach your desired dreams unless you take chances. Every time you take a chance, you are risking something. The most important advancements throughout history, whether social, technological, medical, or educational, etc., happened because people were willing to go beyond their comfort zone and build something new, despite any pushback, obstacles, or criticism.

Going beyond your comfort zone can include:

- Applying for a new job.
- Starting a business.
- Moving to a new location.
- Traveling to a place you have never been before.
- Trying something new, in general.
- Making new friends.

Even leaving your home every day, driving in your car, or eating at a restaurant all have elements of vulnerability to them.

Vulnerability Results In Increased Abilities

People who embrace vulnerability do not fear the unknown. At the very least, they do not let the unknown stop them. They strive to learn and do whatever they can to become better. Anything they can't do is viewed as a challenge that needs to be overcome, rather than something insurmountable. People in this category can also become bored easily. Therefore, they need to set new goals regularly to keep growing. When you are vulnerable:

- You will take that extra training that is required for work.
- You will try something new, possibly make a mistake, and then learn from it.
- Ask someone for help when you are struggling.
- Get guidance from a person who may be more knowledgeable than you on a subject.

Vulnerability Allows Opening Up To Others

When you are vulnerable, you are more open to others because you are willing to put your emotions on the line. This can lead to more compatible relationships because people will know what you like and are about. You will attract real friends and partners who will stick by your side. Being open with superficial friends who are only there during the good times can help weed out all of these toxic relationships. When fake friends know about your internal struggles, they are not as confident that you will always be successful, which will result in them abandoning the ship. Here are some ways that vulnerability allows you to open up:

- Letting the person who you've had a crush on, know exactly how you feel.
- Asking for a raise or promotion at work.
- Expressing your feelings when someone is upsetting you.

Vulnerability Makes You More Comfortable With Discomfort

When you enter into a state of vulnerability, it makes you uncomfortable. You are exposing yourself to potential harm and ridicule, which is not an easy thing to take. It puts you in a state of discomfort, and when it happens the first time, it is extremely difficult. When you make yourself vulnerable again, it is still hard, but slightly easier. Do it three, four, or five more times, and suddenly, it is not that bad. Don't get me wrong. Discomfort is never fun, but the more you get used to it, the more comfortable you get with it. Every time you make yourself vulnerable, you put yourself in a state of discomfort, and the more often it occurs, the more comfortable you will be.

Simply put: Vulnerability makes you more comfortable with discomfort.

Being vulnerable has its advantages. In fact, it is nearly impossible to succeed and progress forward if you don't make yourself vulnerable often. Growth does not happen inside of a comfort zone. If you are ready to grow, start taking chances, and put yourself in a state of vulnerability. Discard that myth that the only way to be tough is to hold your guard up. True courage comes when you let your guard down. Think of vulnerability as a muscle. The more you do it, the stronger it will become.

How To Make Yourself Vulnerable

Now that we know the benefits of being vulnerable, I will discuss some ways to transition to this mindset. This will help you if you ever choose to seek out professional help because you will be more willing to express yourself and all of your concerns. This means that more progress will be made during any therapy, coaching, or counseling sessions. The following are some ways to make yourself a more vulnerable person.

Define Vulnerability For Yourself

Before you can become vulnerable, you must define what it means to you. When you think of vulnerability, what comes to your mind? Is it a sign of strength, like we discussed above, or is it still viewed as being weak? What was the perception of vulnerability in your home growing up? This perception could also be impacting your opinion right now. Once you understand what vulnerability means to you, you now have an opportunity to redefine it if needed.

Get To Know Yourself Better

You must understand yourself on a deeper level in order to become more vulnerable. A good way to do this is to anchor yourself to where you are on a daily basis by becoming more mindful. Mindfulness allows you to be present in your current situation, rather than focusing on the past or present. This will give you a sense of how you're feeling at the moment. I went over some mindfulness techniques in an earlier chapter. If you can get involved with yoga or meditation, they can be very beneficial for you. Regular activities like listening to music or writing can be helpful in this regard too. These exercises to anchor ourselves are sometimes all we need to become comfortable in our vulnerability.

Talk To Yourself In The Mirror

Giving yourself a good pep talk in the mirror can help crack open your emotions, so you become more forthcoming with yourself and other people. This may seem strange or uncomfortable at first, but that is what vulnerability is all about. Talk to yourself in the mirror and even regularly, if possible.

Get Familiar With Feeling Vulnerable

Vulnerability can be challenging for those who are not used to it. Trying to become this way can become quite awkward. This is why you must ease into it. Instead of avoiding or numbing your uncomfortable emotions, let yourself actually feel them. Notice how your mind and body handle them after a while. This will build up some immunity for you. Once you become more comfortable with vulnerability, it will be easier to enter this state on a regular basis. This goes along with becoming comfortable with discomfort.

Push Yourself Outside Of Your Comfort Zone

This is when you have to start taking real action. Start doing things, whatever they may be, that forces you out of your comfort zone. This is how you make yourself vulnerable. Start small by engaging in little activities you have never done before and made you slightly uncomfortable. From there, keep going even further. Do something every day that challenges you. Some examples include:

- Eating a new type of food.
- Going to a new spot in the evening you have never been to before.
- Applying for a new job.
- Joining some type of social group.

- Going up to someone and talking to them randomly.
- Working out at the gym.
- Taking dance lessons.
- Performing in a theatrical performance.

Anything that makes you uncomfortable is fair game here. This is not exclusive to activities. If you have a tendency to behave in a certain manner, you can change your behavior to take yourself out of your comfort zone. For example, if you tend to become defensive easily, the next time you have these feelings coming on, try taking a deep breath and acting differently. When you feel the physical sensations in your body telling you not to do these things, then you will know you are vulnerable. Keep going at this point, and do not stop. This is when actual growth is happening, which can be a painful experience.

Start Sharing Your Truth

When you are vulnerable, you are more likely to express your truth, whether it is good or bad. Expressing your love for someone puts you in a position to possibly be shut down, and telling someone what you dislike about them puts you in a position of judgment. Whatever thoughts and feelings are going through you, learn to start expressing them. If someone upset you, let them know. If someone did something kind to make you happy, let them know that too. Of course, there is a time and place for all of this, but when that time and place is right, go for it.

Take Responsibility For Your Thoughts

We are all responsible for our actions, but we are also responsible for our thoughts. We must own our emotions, rather than blaming it on someone else. We cannot control what happens outside of us, but we can control how we react to those things. When you take responsibility, you are breaking down your defenses and letting people see the whole you. This also shows how much power you actually have over your life. When something in your environment happens that's beyond your control, the fact that you are able to control your thoughts and feelings shows tremendous strength and control.

Practice All The Time

Just like anything else, becoming vulnerable takes extreme practice. The more and more you put yourself out there, the easier it becomes. Eventually, it will become natural.

What Is A Life Coach?

Life Coaching

Life coaching is not a well-known industry yet. Even though there are many life coaches out there who are heavily successful, like Tony Robbins, John Maxwell, and Brian Tracy, the general public is largely unaware of what they can do. However, many high-level people have been using life coaches for years, which may be why they are in their current position. Coaches are an instrumental part of helping people realize their goals and create the life they desire. They do not tell people what to do but rather help their clients explore and discover the answers within themselves. Life coaches are different from therapists in that they don't treat mental health disorders in any way. They simply work with clients to help them build a better future.

Life coaches have many tools and techniques at their disposal. The most important thing is that they are great listeners and know how to ask the right questions to really get you to think. When you work with a life coach, you will truly see things from a different perspective. It is always important to have support, and a life coach will give it to you in every way. What makes them different from a friend or family member is that they provide an objective perspective of your situation without any judgment. This can be beneficial when trying to get real answers on what to do. The following are some major signs that you may need the assistance of a life coach:

You Feel Lost, In General

With all of the things going on in the world and trying to keep it all balanced, it can be easy to become lost and confused. There are too many things to take care of, and the more time we spend not finding balance, the more lost we become. When you get to the point that you don't know where you are or what you want, you need to seek out some professional help. Working with a life coach is a great starting point to start reorganizing your life and creating a new journey.

You Have A Lot Of Self-doubts

Self-doubt has been known to kill many dreams. You can have all of the talent and resources in the world, but if you don't believe in yourself, you will eventually fall apart. Many people know what they want in their lives, but so many environmental factors and internal emotions come into play, and we end up becoming confused and uncertain. This uncertainty can lead to a lot of self-doubts and low confidence. A life coach can help you overcome self-doubt and guide you in realizing your dreams.

You Have a Goal, But No Idea How To Reach It

It's actually easy to come up with a goal. You just have to have a vision for what you want in the future. You can come up with this right away. However, knowing how to get there is a different story. For example, you may have a vision of owning a home on the lake but no idea how to make it a reality. What action steps should you take after creating your goal or vision? A life coach is a perfect person to help you figure this out. They can guide you in coming up with a strategic plan to get you where you want to be. Once you start working with a coach, the vision you have in your mind will soon be in front of you.

Many great ideas go unrealized because people have no clarity or organization to start moving forward. Instead, the plan becomes lost in an array of mass confusion, never to be found again. If you have ideas floating around in your head, don't let them go to waste. Seek out the assistance of a life coach so your vision can become a reality.

You Want To Change Careers

If you are at the point of needing to find something new, a life coach can help guide you in the right direction. Whether it's changing careers, changing positions, or starting a business, having a strong support system that can lead you to the right answers is invaluable. The expertise of a life coach can give you much confidence and reassurance to take the necessary steps.

Business coaches are a subset of life coaches, and they can help you much more thoroughly in this area.

You Need To Improve Your Health

Another subset of life coaching is health coaching. A coach in this arena can help you with meal planning based on your specific metabolism. It can be hard to determine this on your own, so a health coach can guide you much faster.

Following Through Is Hard For You

If you make goals and get started on them but then quit while you are ahead, you have a problem with following through. If you make promises to other people and then go back on your word, you also have a problem with following through. Basically, if you have a reputation for never doing what you say you will, whether it's to yourself or someone else, you need to fix your attitude because you are harming more than just yourself.

A good life coach can hold you accountable for what you say, so you do not downplay your obligations. They will be there to make sure you follow through on everything, from goals, actions, to promises. You will feel better about yourself if you honor your word.

You Procrastinate

If you delay important tasks unnecessarily, you are a procrastinator, and this is not a good habit to get into. Putting things off until later, which can be taken care of now, can lead to many consequences, including poor productivity and missed opportunities. Reaching your goals requires discipline, action, and getting things done on a deadline. Procrastination ensures none of these traits exists.

A life coach can help you change your patterns of behavior, which will lead to new habit formation. Once you break the habit of procrastination, you will start accomplishing what you set out to do well ahead of time. Stop putting off important tasks because you don't feel like dealing with them. You will have to at some point.

You Are Always Stressed

If you are someone who becomes stressed easily, trying to live life without any support will only make things worse. Instead, seek out a life coach, and you will save a lot of time and energy, which will prevent burnout. A life coach can provide the support you need to feel less stressed about things. They can also shed some clarity on your path and show you some effective relaxation techniques, like mindfulness methods. Stress can have many consequences down the line and can deteriorate you physically, mentally, spiritually, and emotionally. It's important not to let it get out of hand.

You Need Better Finances

While a life coach will not be able to give you tips on stocks, what type of career is best for you, or any financial advice whatsoever, they can guide you in the right direction towards resources that can help you. You will get the insight you need by finding your own answers in a more profitable direction. The clarity and guidance a life coach will provide for you will result in many rewards down the line.

As you can see, going to see a life coach does not mean you will be given the answers. You will be guided in discovering your own answers, and these are where the best solutions come from. As you progress forward, you will gain a lot of self-confidence through these measures. Knowing that you had it in you all along is one of the beauties of working with a life coach. I mentioned some of these already, but life coaching has several subsets, like:

- Business coaching
- Spiritual coaching
- Time management coaching
- Relationship coaching

What Is A Licensed Therapist?

Therapy

There are actually many types of licensed therapists who work in different specialties. There are some who are more generalized but depending on what you need help with, going to someone who is more specialized might be the better route. For example, there are therapists who deal with marriage and family issues; others help with addiction, some help with living conditions, and some work with people who have developmental disabilities, etc. While I don't know what specific issues in your life you need help with, I do know that someone is out there to assist you if you need it.

Unlike a life coach, therapists work with people who have mental health disorders or very deep emotional issues. Life coaches, more or less, work with a healthy population who simply need guidance in finding the answers to life's problems. Therapists work with individuals dealing with more serious issues overall. They have more sophisticated methods of dealing with distress, including psychotherapy, which comes in various forms. Once again, seeking out help in this manner is not a form of weakness but rather a strength. You are brave enough to put your emotions out there and welcome the feedback you need. A licensed therapist can certainly do what a life coach can, but it is not usually their specialty. It is better to reserve seeing a therapist for some of the following issues.

You're Having Difficulty Regulating Your Emotions

Everyone feels sad, anxious, stressed, or overwhelmed at some point in their lives. In some cases, these emotions can get out of control for a while during times of total distress, like the loss of a loved one or a major life change. This is natural and nothing to become alarmed about.

Some individuals have a hard time regulating their emotions on a regular basis, and they are out of control most of the time. Uncontrolled emotions may be hiding a deeper mental health issue. For example, chronic anger could be the result of underlying depression, and the person does not know any other way to express it. The same can be true of sadness and anxiety that becomes chronic. They might be what's showing on the outside, but not revealing what is happening inside.

A licensed therapist can dig deeper into the emotional regulation issues. There could be several underlying reasons for negative emotions to constantly popping up, and some may be rooted in the person's history, like childhood trauma or past abusive relationship. A therapist can intervene before an individual turns to reckless behavior and can even assist when they've already reached this point.

Your Performance At Work Or School Is Not Effective

This could be something handled by a life coach if it's an issue with procrastination, time management, or other nonclinical problems. However, this can also be related to deeper mental or psychological issues that impair attention, concentration, memory, and energy. All of this can lead to apathy, which impairs the drive to enjoy work. Obviously, if your work productivity is poor, it not only affects you but those who rely on you, as well.

Through seeking the help of a therapist, you can start to self-regulate your behavior through various problems solving and relaxation strategies. These various methods can also target the root of your emotional setbacks and help you start enjoying life again, including work.

Disruptions In Sleep Or Appetite

The most common things we do every day, like eating and sleeping, can be severely disrupted by mental health issues. It can impact us in a variety of ways, depending on the disorder in question. For example, being in a manic state can result in difficulty sleeping, while being sad or depressed can lead to sleeping too much. The same holds true for eating. A person can start eating too much or not enough because of a mental health problem they are facing.

If you notice changes in any of these areas on a long-term basis, it might be time to assess what is happening in your life. If you are unable to figure it out on your own, definitely seek out the help of a professional.

Your Struggling With Relationships

Struggling to build and maintain relationships can be another sign of poor mental health. We may pull away from people who are closest to us for no apparent reason, have a lot of insecurities, or even start overly relying on people for emotional support. While there's nothing wrong with leaning on people once in a while, you must also be able to stand on your own and deal with life's issues.

Individuals with deeper emotional issues can also have difficulty with developing relationships at work or in their personal lives. Trying to work in a team or communicating with anybody can seem impossible. This will take a toll on existing relationships and make it hard to create new relationships in the future. Remember that cultivating bonds with other people is needed to feel good in life. Even introverts cannot be alone all the time.

While you don't have to be friends with everyone you meet, having the right relationships in life is imperative for personal wellbeing. A skilled therapist can teach you proper social skills, like assertiveness, while also managing your underlying mental health issues.

You've Experienced Trauma

Trauma may be emotional, mental, or physical, and can be the result of many things, like abuse, neglect, or witnessing something horrific. Many individuals have not recovered from their past trauma because they suppressed it in some way. People in this situation can benefit greatly from talk therapy, which is psychotherapy. There are many forms of psychotherapy that can be used to explore the painful experiences of a person and determine exactly what they are going through.

A therapist can provide a confidential space that is free from judgment do their clients can fully express themselves and what is going on. The client also does not have to worry about protecting the therapist by telling them about their experiences. A strong therapist can help their clients develop new ways of perceiving their trauma and learn new techniques to break the association with an event. While the trauma will never go away completely, it won't have the same power over someone like it did before.

Activities You Once Enjoyed Are No Longer Appealing

People who are struggling with emotional issues often feel disconnected from life, which causes them to be act alienated. As a result, they lose interest in the activities they once loved, like hobbies or social gatherings. They even isolate themselves from people they were once very close to. Individuals who once had goals and dreams of doing great things can start feeling a lot of apathy towards their future. In extreme cases, they start wishing they weren't alive. This does not necessarily mean they are suicidal, but they would not mind going to bed and not waking up the next morning.

Once again, a licensed therapist can help in a tremendous way with situations like this. Therapy can help someone figure out what's holding them back, get rid of negative thoughts, and reconnect with the things that bring joy.

You're Grieving

While it's natural to grieve during periods of sadness, like the loss of a loved one, going through a divorce, getting fired from a job, or being diagnosed with a chronic illness, it can still weight heavily on a person if many bad events occur in a short period of time. If you have no one to share the emotional burden with, the ordeal can be much more difficult. Grief counseling can provide a safe space for someone going through major life events that are too overwhelming to deal with alone. Having a compassionate place for a person to express their grievances and process their emotions can go a long way.

Your Physical Health Is Going Down

Despite the progress made with mental health, it is still not given nearly the same amount of attention as physical health, which is a huge mistake. Mental health and physical health are interconnected in so many ways, and having a decline in one can lead to a decline in the other. Mental health issues like anger, depression, sadness, and anxiety have many effects on physical health. In the first place, they can radically change someone's behavior. Eating disorders, poor nutrition, lack of physical activity, altered sleep patterns, and delaying health checkups can all be the result of some type of mental health disorder.

Furthermore, various emotions can cause our bodies to release various hormones that can have damaging effects over time, like heart issues or diabetes. The stress that comes from mental health can lead to many health consequences. Suppose you find yourself dealing with physical health problems and have no idea why you should be getting checked out anyway. Make sure you are getting assessed for any mental health issues too.

Finally, physical health has an effect on mental health too. Dealing with a new chronic illness, unhealthy weight gain, poor diet, and lack of exercise can all lead back to emotional issues, which, in turn, will result in further physical complications. It is a vicious cycle to get caught up in.

You Are Turning To An Activity As A Coping Mechanism

When we are under emotional distress, we often turn to things we find rewarding, numbing, or distracting to take our minds off the pain. These are strategies that are used to cope. The activities we engage in can often be destructive, like substance abuse or high-risk activities we are not used to. All of these things can help alleviate the pain in the short term but will not fix the root cause of our issues. In fact, engaging in these behaviors only prolongs the agony because we put ff facing our problems.

If you find yourself turning to substances or other harmful activities, it's time to seek out help. Further treatment is necessary for these instances to help fix any underlying issues that are not known.

A licensed therapist can be a number of things, like a counselor, clinical psychologist, or social worker. There is a lot of crossover in these roles, but they also have their own unique strengths, as well. To determine who the best therapist is for you, do your research and find the one who is dedicated to helping you with your issues.

A Psychologist vs. Psychiatrist

People are confused between these two professions; however, there is a difference between a psychologist, or therapist, versus a psychiatrist. They are both mental health professionals but have different approaches to the field. A psychologist is not a medical doctor. Their focus is more on talk therapy or psychotherapy. Since they cannot prescribe medications, they have to rely on many non-medical techniques to help their clients.

Psychiatrists, on the other hand, must go to medical school and become medical doctors. As a result, they take a much more medically-based approach to healing their clients, like prescribing medications or engaging in electroconvulsive therapy, which involves some electrical stimulation of the brain under anesthesia for people suffering from extreme depression or bipolar disorder.

A psychiatrist can do what a psychologist does, but in most instances, a trained psychologist will be more experienced with psychotherapy because much of their practice is based on it. People visit psychiatrists when suffering from much more severe cases of mental health disorders that psychotherapy and other non-medical treatments do not work for.

The bottom line here is that there are many ways to get professional help if needed. If you are not feeling well and don't know how to get out of this trap, never hesitate to seek out help due to fear or negative stigmas. Remember that you are stronger for getting help and making yourself vulnerable than you are by holding everything in.

Chapter 7: The Advantages Of Feeling Good

I have been talking about feeling good, and the many ways people can enter this state of mind. There is a reason people want to feel good. It gives them so many advantages in every area of their lives. No matter what activity you engage in or what path you decide to take, you will perform better when you are feeling good. The focus of this chapter will be to discuss the many advantages of feeling good and the various ways the different aspects of our lives are affected positively. It always feels good to feel good.

Feeling Good!

Feeling Good At Work

When people feel good and are full of positive emotions, they are better off at work or place of business. This is why so many companies have adjusted over the years to make their environments more friendly and less toxic. Employee incentives and wellness programs have become powerful tools to improve overall employee well-being. I will go over some exceptional ways that feeling good gives you multiple advantages in the workplace.

Better Health And Stress Management

When you genuinely feel good at work, you recover faster from the damage done by negative emotions. Which means you get over stressful situations more easily. Happier people tend to bounce back faster than unhealthy people. This faster recovery leads to improved productivity because people are not wasting their time remembering what made them feel bad. They have already gotten past it and moved onto the next task or project.

Positivity, happiness, and feeling good is also associated with a better immune system. This results in fewer call-offs from work because you are not stricken with illness as often. There is a strong link between feeling good and improved health and better stress management, which will reflect well in the workplace.

Enhance Relationships and Creativity

You are not required to be friends with or even like the people you work with. However, you must have a working relationship with them; otherwise, nothing will get accomplished. A working relationship means you are willing to be a team for the betterment of the company and whatever projects you may be working on. When you are happy and feel good, you are more likely to get along with other people. Even if you don't get along with them, you are able to ignore these emotions long enough to get the work done. Emotions will rub off on other people too. If you show positive emotions, like happiness at work, soon enough, other people will start becoming happier too.

Your creativity will shine through, as well. When you feel lousy, your mind becomes clouded, and you are not able to think straight. Feeling good comes with more clarity of the mind, which allows you to come up with better ideas. To create your best work, you have to be somewhat creative, and being happy leads to higher creativity.

Creativity leads to a lot of innovation in business. All of the greatest products from every industry are around because of innovative ideas from some great minds.

Greater Job Satisfaction

If you genuinely feel good, your job satisfaction will also go up. Even if it's not your dream job, you will still love being there because you will make the best of the situation. When people are happier at work, there will be less chance of burnout and leaving the company. Many employees do not leave because the work is too hard. They leave because of a toxic work environment. If more people are satisfied with their companies, there is much less chance of a toxic environment.

Happiness Leads To Health

Being a healthy person, overall, can lead to more happiness, and in turn, happiness can lead to better health. While there are other factors at play, like lifestyle and genetics, feeling good, or being happy, correlates in many ways to improved health outcomes. They both go hand-in-hand. I have covered some of these topics already but will get more in-depth into how feeling good is linked to good health. This will give you much more motivation to take care of your well-being.

It Protects Your Heart

Being happy and feeling good is great for your heart health. Happiness has been shown to reduce the risk of heart disease in many sample studies. For example, a study of over 6,500 participants over the age of 65 found that positive well-being was connected to a nine percent lower risk of high blood pressure. A number of other studies have shown that being in a good state of mind reduces the risk of heart disease by 13-16%. While more research is needed, there is a pretty good indication that being a happy person in general and feeling good is associated with improved heart health. So, laugh often and smile more, and you will be helping your heart out in a small way.

Increased Life Expectancy

There was a long-term study that was published in 2015, which studied the effects of happiness on survival rates in 32,000 people over a 30 years period. The findings suggested that the risk of earlier death was 14% higher in unhappy individuals than happy individuals who felt good. A variety of other studies looked at the association between positive well-being and longevity in both healthy individuals and those with underlying health conditions. Once again, the results showed increased survival rates in those who were happier as the rate of death was reduced by 2% in people with pre-existing conditions and 18% in those who were healthy.

It is not known why happiness leads to higher life expectancy, but the countless studies done over the years seem to favor this conclusion. Of course, further studies need to be done. A major reason could be the increase in beneficial behaviors, like improved diet, more physical activity, and less destructive behaviors, like smoking or drinking. In summary, happier people seem to live longer.

Reduce Pain

Higher well-being may reduce pain and stiffness related to arthritis, which causes inflammation and degeneration of the joints. Once again, several studies have shown a reduction in pain, but the reasons behind it are not completely clear. Researchers suggest that happier people have a broader perspective on life and what it has to offer, and this leads to more effective coping strategies that reduce the perception of pain.

Promotes A Healthier Lifestyle

Being a happy person promotes a wide-range of lifestyle habits that are important for overall health. Happy people tend to eat food that is more nutritious and also ration their portion sizes more carefully. Their food tends to be more nutrient-dense, as well. A person who is feeling good will more likely prepare a fresh meal rather than go to a fast-food restaurant.

In a study of 7,000 adults, it was found that people with a positive well-being were 33% more likely to be physically active. Regular physical activity builds strong bones, improves energy levels, reduces blood pressure, and gets rid of excess body fat.

Being happy will also improve other habits, like better sleep, more socializing with friends, increased performance, and less time in front of the television. Most people who are happy will opt to spend time in nature, consuming fresh air over anything negative on the news or social media.

Boosts The Immune System

A healthy immune system is essential to maintain health. Our immune systems are working 24/7 to make sure our bodies do not get taken over by a wealth of diseases that are waiting to pounce on all of our internal cells, tissues, and organs. Our immune system is our internal army fighting to keep us protected from various pathogens.

Various studies have shown that being happy boosts our immune system function, effectively improving our ability to fight off infections and diseases. This may be due to the impact that happiness has on the HPA axis, which regulates the immune system, along with hormones, digestion, and stress levels.

Once again, happy people are more likely to partake in health-promoting behaviors that also boost the immune system. You may notice that you'll get the cold and feel lousy much less often when you are a happy person.

Feeling Good And Relationships

People who feel good will naturally think more positively. Those who think positively will have better relationships. This is because they are able to connect with others in a more mutually beneficial way. I will go over some significant reasons why people who feel good have better relationship outcomes. Learn to take a more positive approach with your relationships.

Feeling Good Attracts Other Good Things

Yes, feeling good attracts other good things in life, including relationships. When you are negative and feeling down, you will also attract more of these feelings, which can lead to self-sabotage. However, feeling good and having a positive approach can lead to richer relationships. If you want to make more connections, you need to first believe that you are deserving of these types of bonds. After this, you can start imagining yourself enjoying these positive relationships. Eventually, they will start coming to you. Remember that people are attracted to those who display a positive vibe.

Feeling Good Helps You Come Up With Solutions

When you feel good, you are much more creative. The benefits of this are not exclusive to work or business. Being creative in relationships is a large benefit too. Feeling good gives you a positive attitude towards life, and positivity increases your creative juices. Every relationship faces adversity, and those who are not in a positive state of well-being will often give up and throw a relationship away over small issues.

On the other hand, when you feel good, you will come up with constructive ways to overcome adversity. With whatever setbacks are occurring within a relationship, having a belief that things can improve is the initial step to creating lasting change.

Feeling Good Results In More Empathy

People who are feeling good are usually living in a chronic pity-party. Their focus usually is on them and their misery. When a person feels good, they have a positive mindset, which results in them understanding other people's perspective much more. Having empathy is definitely beneficial in romantic relationships because it will promote more closeness and intimacy. A relationship cannot be one-sided, and this is generally the case when one of the parties is not in a good state of well-being. Over time, this will lead to both members lacking empathy because people can only care about others for so long before it starts getting old.

Feeling Good Leads To Being Better At Conflict Resolution

Do you think that relationships are not full of conflict? Well, that's a major misconception because all relationships have them, no matter how good they are. When a person does not feel good, they are less likely to want to deal with conflict and will let it fester. Negative people are not interested in solving problems and are more likely to just worry about them. When arguments occur, they are highly unproductive and lead to more strife.

A person who is in a positive state of well-being is more likely to resolve issues that come up. Conflicts are bound to arise in a relationship, and positive thinkers can deal with the stress in a rational way. This is much more productive and beneficial than ignoring the problem or blowing it out of proportion. If there is a disagreement between two people who are feeling good at the moment, the conflict will be resolved much more quickly and will more likely favor both sides.

Feeling Good Means, You Will Be Better Company

Being around someone who is gloomy, negative, and always acting like the victim can become distressing after a while. No one wants to be around someone who makes them feel this way. When you are in a positive state of well-being, you exude better vibes, and this will be more attractive to other people, including your partner. Your partner will want to spend more quality time with you when you are feeling good, as opposed to being negative.

The Law Of Attraction

The Law of Attraction is an ability one has to attract positive things in their lives. Following this law can help ensure that you feel good every day, and therefore, you will attract good from the universe. The basis of the Law of Attraction is that whatever thoughts you put out into the universe will ultimately come back to you through an attraction. For example, if you put out happiness into the universe, you will get happiness back.

Our minds work like a magnet. The ideas that we think about are what the universe hears. Therefore, we must be very careful about how we think and what we think about because the universe is listening. The tricky part is that even if you are thinking about something in a negative manner, you will still attract it. For example, if you are thinking about not being in a state of poverty, the fact that poverty is on your mind means that those are the signals you are sending out into the world. It is better not to think about poverty at all and only think about wealth.

Sadly, too many people are not aware of the power of their thoughts, so they leave them unchecked. This will send out the incorrect messages that you don't want and result in attracting more negativity into your life.

There is some confusion about the Law of Attraction. It does not mean that if you think about money that it will naturally fall from the sky. That is not how the law works. Instead, when you think about money and wealth, the universe will hear this and lead you to opportunities to create more wealth. It is still your job to recognize those opportunities and take advantage of them.

Even if someone does not fully believe in the Law of Attraction, there is no denying that putting positive vibes out into the world is more productive than putting out negative vibes. The Law of Attraction has existed in some form, or another, throughout the world for many centuries. Various cultures and religions have believed in some variation of it. In modern times, many philosophers, scientists, business professionals, and other people of prominence have vouched for the validity of the law.

Many individuals have a hard time accepting the Law of Attraction because it points to the fact that each individual shaped the decisions that they've made in life, and therefore, their success. However, once you understand the power of the law, you can be renewed with hope and courage that you are free to take charge of your life. Knowing that you have control can be a freeing moment for many.

When you learn to use the Law of Attraction to your favor, that is when you can start feeling good. By knowing how the law works, you can begin to visualize exactly the type of life you want to live and the steps you need to take to get you there. If you don't like your current picture, then start painting a new one. If your goal is to simply feel good, picture ways to make this happen for you and take the necessary action. The universe will be on your side if you know how to use it.

The Law of Attraction can be utilized in the following ways:

- Manifest love and relationships by imaging your perfect partner and always keeping that picture at the forefront of your mind.
- Attract money and wealth by picturing what that looks like for you. For example, imagine yourself at a large table with tons of food, living in a big house with plenty of space, or traveling to a far-off destination. Whatever wealth means to you, start imagining it.
- Improve your physical and mental health by training your brain to see the positive things in life.

Once you start using the Law of Attraction, you will notice your life-changing in amazing ways. When you start imagining what feeling good means to you, you can start working towards it.

The Ways To Approach Life

The way our life turns out has a lot to do with how we approach it. The way we view things plays a major role in how we move forward. Just like how beauty lies in the eyes of the beholder, how we view life is the way it becomes. The following are some different approaches one can take.

The Hedonic Approach

This type of approach involved people who put their own guilty pleasures before anything else. This means they will do whatever they can, and even harm others in the process, just to satisfy one of their cravings. They cannot help themselves in this manner. These individuals take an egocentric attitude when it comes to life. These guilty pleasures do not have to be highly sinful. They can be things like eating a whole cake late at night, binge-watching an entire show on Netflix, or oversleeping excessively on the weekends. Those who take the hedonic approach simply want to feel pleasure, even if it's harming them in the long run.

The Rat Race Approach

This is another egocentric approach that involves being competitive. When you follow the rat race approach, you are concerned about what's best for you and nothing else. Your entire goal is to win at all costs. This is a selfish path that people take because as long as they are helping themselves, nobody else's wellbeing really matters.

The Nihilistic Approach

This is a completely pessimistic approach that centers around indulging in negative thought patterns. This is mostly seen in individuals who are highly depressed or stressed out. A nihilist cannot divert their attention away from the worries and mishaps in life, and they lack any type of inspiration to reconcile their negative emotions. Someone who takes this approach is likely to deal with many emotional issues that need to be overcome.

The Positive Approach

This is believed to be the best approach that leads to happiness, contentment, and feeling good. People who follow this pathway are able to uncover the right balance between wanting something and needing something. They also focus on building their good qualities. Let's be real for a moment. Not everything we have in life is a necessity. Somethings, they are just things we want or have for convenience. This is okay, as long as we aren't controlled by them. The positive approach is focused on solutions, is goal-oriented, and a direct pathway to happiness in life.

It's rare that a person only follows one of these approaches during their life. In most cases, it is a combination of all of them, and it really depends on what part of their life we are referring to or what their current mental status is. For example, a person can take the rat race approach when it comes to working but take the positive approach when they are at home. Also, a person may have been more of a nihilist when they were younger or going through certain stages in life, but not have a positive approach as they've gotten older.

The approach you decide to take determines whether you are truly feeling good or not.

Why should you strive to feel good? You will simply live a better life when you do. Think about your past and remember all of the times you felt good and how much of an improvement it was in your life. Even though I don't know you personally, I am certain that everything you went through in life was easier when you were in a positive state of well-being. The major goal you should have every day is to feel good. When you feel good, everything else starts falling into place and becoming clearer. When you don't feel good, every obstacle or challenge seems insurmountable.

Chapter 8: Feeling Good In Real Life

All of the previous chapters in this book have discussed the idea of feeling good. I have gone over what this concept means and how we can all realize it in our own lives. When you feel good, every area of your life is positively affected. With the same token, this is also the case when you feel bad. The focus of this chapter will be going over some hypothetical stories concerning real-life situations and showing you how much better a circumstance can be handled when a person is feeling good versus when they are not. While these stories are not real, I will use real names to help the stories flow better.

Mike's Story

Mike is stranded on the side of the road and needs to take care of several things to get moving. The following are two separate stories on how the situation can be handled when Mike is feeling good and when he is not feeling good.

Not Feeling Good

Mike was driving down the highway when his car suddenly started shaking uncontrollably. He was safely able to pull over to the side of the road and get out of harm's way. Luckily, the highway was not too busy at this time, so he was able to change lanes quite easily.

Mike had already had a rough day and was just ready to go home and take a nap. The day was full of tasks that kept on coming, and he had no idea how to handle them all. His diet consisted of food he got from the vending machine because he did not have time to sit down and eat his lunch. By the time his car became stranded on the side of the road, Mike was completely overwhelmed with everything else and had to ability to focus.

As a result, he just sat there in the front seat with his head on the steering wheel. He was trying to figure out what to do next but could not come up with an idea. Since the highway was not busy, nobody really stopped to see if he was okay. Mike did not even think about getting out and waving someone down.

After several minutes, Mike called a tow truck, which arrived about 45 minutes later. The total charge was well over $100, and it was going to be towed to a mechanic that Mike was not familiar with. After this, Mike called for a cab to drive him home, and he would have to go see his car in the morning.

The next morning, he left early and arrived just as the dealership was opening up. After taking care of the paperwork, Mike left to go back home because he was tired. He just wanted to sleep the entire day while waiting for his car. On the way home, Mike realized the mistake he just made. He completely forgot that his insurance covers towing, and he also had a warranty for repairs with the dealership. Through all of the confusion going on in his mind, he completely forgot about all of this. As soon as he got home, he called his insurance company. Unfortunately, they could not do anything for him because he already paid for the towing. His dealership also could not help him because he already authorized the repairs at the other mechanic's shop.

Since Mike was tired and could not think clearly, he made a major mistake that cost him a lot of money. If he had taken a few extra minutes to think everything through, he could have made the proper decisions related to his car. After this, Mike felt even worse than he already did.

Feeling Good

Mike was driving down the road when his car began shaking uncontrollably. He quickly pulled over to the side of the road, which was easy because the highway was fairly empty. After pulling over, Mike looked around to make sure everything was safe before getting out of the car. He assessed for any damage or leaks and then sat back in the car. Luckily, he had just eaten a nice meal before leaving work, so he wasn't hungry.

He thought for a minute about what he should do next and suddenly remembered having towing service as part of his insurance. He also remembered that his dealership offered him a warranty, and his car was still within the mileage limit. After calling his insurance company, he called his dealership to let them know he would be bringing the car over there.

The tow truck showed up, and he was able to ride with them to the dealership. After getting his car checked in, Mike also followed up on getting a rental car until his own car was ready again. Lucky for him, all of this was covered under the services he had, and it was a good thing he was lucky enough to remember that.

After a few days, Mike was able to pick up his car again and take it home. He paid no extra money for all of the services he had done.

Mike's story shows that feeling good can make dealing with inconveniences like his much easier to deal with. In the earlier scenario, since Mike was not feeling good and his mind was completely bogged down, he made some poor decisions that cost him quite a bit. In the second scenario, he was able to think with much more clarity.

Jennifer's Story

Jennifer works for a busy office, and there are many projects that need to be completed.

Not Feeling Good

Jennifer has been working hard for several days, trying to take care of all the items on her checklist. She went to bed late the night before because she spent several hours at a friend's house and she arrived home late. As a result, she also woke up late, missed breakfast, and was practically running on empty with nothing but caffeine in her system. As a result, she was completely frazzled all day as she completed her tasks.

About midway through the day, Jennifer was about to burn out completely, so she took in some more coffee. She went back to working on several projects at the same time. She wanted to get them all done by the end of the day. However, because her mind was so preoccupied with everything, she could barely focus her attention on anything.

By the end of the day, Jennifer got absolutely nothing done. She decided to take the work home, so she could finish it by the next day. On the way home, she stopped by a fast food place because she did not want to spend any time preparing food at home. After eating, Jennifer felt tired and went to sleep. She did not wake up until the next day, which means she did not get any of her work done the previous night. She also did not sleep well, as she tossed and turned all night because of the heavy meal she ate right before falling asleep.

Jennifer would now have to work on her projects from the previous day and take home her other tasks to work on in the evening. She had plans to spend time with friends, but she would have to cancel those. This was the third time in the last couple of weeks, and her friends were becoming more concerned and frustrated.

Feeling Good

Jennifer has been working hard for several days to make sure she completes all of the items on her checklist. A few days earlier, she prioritized all of her tasks to make sure all of the important ones get done first. She went out with her friend the night before to decompress after several days of stressful work, but luckily, she excused herself early so she could go home and get a good night's sleep before coming into the work the next day.

She knew there were several things she needed to do, so she got up early and ate breakfast. She needed to have enough fuel to last her during the morning hours. It worked as she was able to efficiently knock the tasks off of her list one at a time. By lunchtime, she was able to stop working and sit down for a while to eat. This gave her more time to settle down for a while.

After she finished her lunch, which consisted of a healthy salad and some grilled chicken, she went back to her desk and began completing the rest of her projects. By the end of the day, she was completely caught up and could go home to relax. There was one more thing to finish, but it was not due for a couple of days, so she started what she could on it and then left it alone until the next day.

Since she was caught up, Jennifer could go home and rest for a while. On the way home, she stopped off at the grocery store so she could make herself a nice meal for dinner. The next morning, she started up again on her tasks and had them done by the end of the day. She had dinner plans at night with some of her friends, and because she kept up on everything, those plans did not have to be canceled.

Jennifer's story shows that feeling good can have a significant impact on a person's career and personal life too. When Jennifer took care of herself and felt good, she performed better in every way, including self-care.

James' Story

Not Feeling Good

James had a busy day ahead of him. There were several tasks on his to-do list, and he had to get them started as soon as possible to get them all done. Unfortunately, he went to bed early the night before, plus had a large meal right before going to bed, so his sleep cycle was thrown off completely. With only a few hours of sleep that was poor anyway, he felt sluggish all day and was not able to engage in any of his tasks.

By the end of the day, he only completed about half of his to-do list and was not highly confident that he performed those tasks well. He would probably have to go back over them the next day. As a result of poor self-care,

James is not way behind on all of his projects and will need to work aggressively to catch up on all of them.

Feeling Good

James had a busy day ahead of him. Since he knew this already, he prepared ahead of time by making sure he got a good night's sleep, so he would have plenty of energy to get through the day. He woke up early and performed some deep breathing exercises to put himself into a state of mindfulness. After this, he had a nice, healthy breakfast to get some extra fuel.

The rest of the day was spent working on the various projects he had on his plate. Every couple of hours, he would take a short break and eat, as well. By the end of the day, he had crossed everything off on his to-do list and was confident he performed them all well. He still had some energy left, so he got a head start on a few things he wasn't planning on starting until the next day. This would save him some time in the future.

James' story shows that if you engage in healthy practices, you will feel good throughout the day and do better work.

Sam's Story

Not Feeling Good

Sam has been feeling sad for a while. He does not want to let anyone know because he is worried about looking weak. His dad always taught him that men never cry, so Sam never does. He goes about his day and never lets anyone know how he is truly feeling. As a result, he has had a lot of rage building up.

Sam has dealt with many different emotions throughout the years, and no matter how good his life was, he never felt truly happy. In fact, he often felt depressed but did not know why. He never wanted to bring it up to anybody. By the time Sam became an adult, he was suffering in silence heavily, which often impacted his work and relationships. He rarely kept friends for a long period of time and never had the chance to date anybody. He was far too anxious on the inside and was worried it would show while talking to a female.

Sam had a difficult time remaining focused at work because he was too busy being worried about what could go wrong. He had no real reason to worry, but he still did. After several years of dealing with emotional issues and holding them all in, Sam had a breakdown and completely isolated himself to his home. He stopped going out for days and even missed several days of work. These were considered unexcused absences. He still did not reach out for help.

After several days of being locked in his home, Sam lost his job and started deteriorating further, in every aspect. He knew there was something going on inside his mind, but he did not know what it was, but he knew he did not want anyone to find out about it.

Feeling Good

Sam has been feeling sad for a while. As a child, he was never allowed to express any emotion because his dad saw this as a sign of weakness. Therefore, Sam always kept everything inside and never asked for help. This began causing him a lot of grief as he got older, and it was starting to affect different areas of his life.

Luckily, when Sam entered the working world, one of his friends noticed what was happening to him. He noticed that Sam wanted to express something but was too stoic to do so. His friend let him know that it showed more strength to express how you feel, rather than bottle everything up. When you hold everything inside, you are in protection mode. When you let your emotions out, you are taking a major risk, which shows courage.

It took a while for Sam to realize this, but he eventually did. After a while, he began opening up about his feelings to a few trusted friends. This helped, but Sam realized there was only so much his friends could do for him. Besides being a listening ear, there was not much else.

One of his friends suggested seeing a counselor to help address any unresolved issues. Sam decided to follow his friend's advice. As a result, he was able to express many of his concerns and get sound advice on how to proceed forward. One of Sam's major concern was finding a relationship. He was too scared to communicate with people over the fear of getting rejected. His counselor was able to help him overcome this fear. As a result, he was able to go out on a few dates.

His performance at work began improving, too, with better productivity and time management skills. After Sam was convinced that it is okay to ask for help, he realized that his dad was wrong all of those years. He realized later that his dad always seemed miserable and suffered from many different illnesses. Sam never understood why but felt that his radical stoicism could have been a contributing factor.

It is better to let your emotions out rather than bottle them all up. If you need the help of a professional, don't be afraid to reach out and get it. Sam's story shows how much better off you can be by going this route.

These hypothetical scenarios are meant to sum up how people can handle various situations when they are not feeling good, compared to when they are. Take the proper steps in your life to improve your well-being because you deserve it.

Conclusion

Thank you for making it through to the end of *(Topic: Feeling Good Therapy)*; let's hope it was informative and able to provide you with all of the tools you need to achieve your goals, whatever they may be. Feeling good is a term that is difficult to define because it means something different to everybody. Of course, if you ask most people if they want to feel good, the answer is a resounding yes. If you go further and ask them what that means, you may get a lot of blank stares.

People want to feel good every day, but because they are confused about how to achieve a positive state of well-being, they often make choices that make them not feel good. This is a problem because these individuals are unknowingly harming themselves. Once people realize that they are not feeling good because of the decisions they are making, they can start engaging in the right actions to create positive changes in their daily lives. By doing this, they will start feeling good.

That was the focus of the previous chapter. After defining what feeling good means in the general sense, the various chapters got into several ways that people don't feel good, physically, mentally, emotionally, and spiritually. In reality, most people do not care for all of these areas in their lives, which is a shame because lagging behind in one aspect can create problems in the others. For example, if you are not doing well mentally, it can negatively affect you physically or emotionally too. I also got into various emotional and mental health disorders that can keep people from not feeling good. These can be a challenge to overcome, but with continuous effort every day, alterations can slowly be made.

After addressing the various ways that can make people not feel good and the damaging effects it can have on their lives, I went over ways to start breaking the chain of being in an unhealthy state of well-being. One of the most important strategies is to start making mindset shifts. Our mindset plays a significant role in how we perceive the world and ourselves. As a result, we need to make sure our mindset is working in our favor. The mindset chapter goes over various methods to start thinking about life differently and creating better results.

In addition to shifting the mindset, self-care needs to become a regular goal for all of us. This is not something that can be placed on the backburner because if we don't care for ourselves, we will eventually fall apart. This won't be good for anybody, and we cannot truly feel good if we don't practice regular self-care activities.

Sometimes, we can resolve our issues on our own or seek out the help of some friends. However, there are other times where we need the help of a professional to get us through the most difficult moments in our lives. A major point in this book is to help people understand that asking for help is not a sign of weakness. On the contrary, it is a sign of strength. Asking for help makes you vulnerable, and vulnerability takes courage. Holding your emotions inside means that you are guarded and not willing to take the risk of looking foolish. Professional help can come in many forms, including life coaching, therapy, counseling, or psychiatry. These various professionals have their own unique traits, but their ultimate goal is to help you in any way they can. Never hesitate to reach out to them for help and guidance.

Finally, the final chapters covered the major advantages of feeling good, which makes all of the effort put into it worthwhile. Whether it is your career, health, personal life, or relationships, being in a positive state of well-being improves the circumstances in every one of these areas. When problems do arise, you will be able to handle them with greater efficiency. When you feel good, you perform better in life, and that's what makes it all worth it.

My hope is that you have a thorough understanding of what feeling good means and how to create it in your own life.

The next step is to take the information in this book and start applying it to every aspect of your life. First, you need to determine what feeling good means to you and then decide if you are currently in the state you want to be in. If the answer is no, you must start taking action to improve your well-being. This should be a goal that is at the forefront of your mind. If you are not feeling good, then you are not doing good, no matter what success you have obtained in life. That is not meant to be put down, but hopefully, it will inspire you to put your well-being as a priority.

Finally, if you found this book useful in any way, a review on Amazon is always appreciated! The more people who know about this book, the more people it will help. My objective is to assist as many people as possible in feeling good through my words, and your positive reviews attract more people to look at this book and become motivated to change.

Choose Joy

www.ingramcontent.com/pod-product-compliance
Lightning Source LLC
Chambersburg PA
CBHW071831080526
44589CB00012B/983